Language of GOD for Little Folks

Level B

Nancy Nicholson

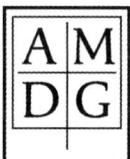

For Little Folks

Christianity...must be made the element and principle of all education...
St. John Henry Newman

Credits

Cover photo: www.gettyimages.com

Illustrated by Nancy Nicholson.

Special thanks to AnneMarie Johnson for the illustrations on pages 15, 16, 19, 22, 23 (sun), 30 (sun), 57 (Jesus and Judas), 58, 71, 86, 89, 93, 100, 102, and 109.

Copyright © 2008, 2005, 1999 Nancy Nicholson   2018 Edition

Language of GOD for Little Folks is under copyright. All rights reserved. No part of this book may be reproduced in any form by any means—electronic, mechanical, or graphic—without prior written permission. Thank you for honoring copyright law.

ISBN: 978-0-9824585-6-3

Printed by Kingery Printing Company
Effingham, Illinois
May 2021

Catholic Heritage Curricula
1-800-490-7713   www.chcweb.com

Table of Contents

Introduction...1
To Listen and Tell...2
The Period and Telling Sentences..3
Sentence Parts...4
Complete Sentences...6
Sentences Start with a Capital Letter..8
Words that Ask...9
Asking and Telling Sentences...10
Sentences that Command 12
Can and May...14
Exclaiming Sentences..15
Review...16
Synonyms...18
Antonyms...21
Homophones..23
Nouns..24
Proper Nouns...26
Capital Letters and God's Name...28
God's Name and Other Titles...29
Review...30
One and More Than One...32
Consonant + y Plurals...34
Possessive Nouns...36
Action Words..39
State of Being Verbs..41
State of Being: Present Tense..42
Action and State of Being..43
State of Being: Present and Past Tense..45
Helping Verbs...47
Review...49
Plurals with Verbs...51
Have and Has...53
Past Tense Verbs with -ed...55

Verbs that Change Form	56
Have and Has as Helpers	57
Past Tense Practice	58
More Verbs that Change Form	59
Subjects: One of Two Sentence Parts	61
Predicates: One of Two Sentence Parts	63
Building Better Sentences	66
Beginning, Middle, and End	68
Review	70
Roots and Verb Endings	72
Suffix Review	76
Prefixes	77
Contractions	79
Syllables	81
Words that Rhyme	82
Don't Give Up	84
Syllable Practice	85
Adjectives: Telling about Nouns	86
Adjectives that Compare	89
Review	91
Pronouns	93
Abbreviations	99
Titles of Respect	102
Initials	103
Abbreviation of States	104
Address Practice	105
Letter Writing	106
Learning about Books	107
Table of Contents	108
Order and the Alphabet	109
Alphabetizing and the Dictionary	112
Review	114
Take My Body, Jesus	116
Appendix: Review Exercises	117
Answer Key	137

Introduction

Language of GOD for Little Folks is designed to provide the Catholic child with a simple introduction to basic English and grammar skills in the context of our Holy Faith. It is also designed with the teacher in mind; no teacher's manual is required because all necessary information, including a removable answer key, is contained within the pages of the student worktext.

Now What Do I Do?

- First, the parent/teacher may read and discuss the page with the child; the child then completes the exercise.

- Next, correct the exercise, using the answer key provided.

- Finally, praise the child for all correct responses. Gently help the child to correct any errors.

It is suggested that two or three workbook pages be completed by the child each week. Because language is a gift both to and from God, it is also strongly suggested that the student be encouraged to use newly-acquired writing skills for His glory. The child may acquire English and grammar practice by writing:

- Simple review exercises: Using books that the child [or family] is currently reading, turn to the first paragraph of any page. With your student, identify punctuation, parts of speech, or rules of grammar that have been studied in the past few weeks.

- Notes to shut-ins, grandparents, priests, religious, and friends

- Brief letters of thanks for mailing to staff of museums, park services, and other points of interest visited on field trips

- Simple journals in which he records daily activities

To Listen and Tell

What fun it is to play with a toddler! When a toddler talks to you, can you understand everything that he says? Do you think that a two-year-old could explain Jesus' Real Presence in Holy Communion? No, because a small child cannot understand the idea. Neither does he have the *vocabulary*, the words, to explain the Real Presence. Some toddlers know and speak a number of words, but they cannot make the words into sentences that can be understood.

Read the sentences below. Do they make sense?

Sunday on we Mass go Holy to. Jesus meet we will there.

Unscramble the words to make sentences. Print the sentences on the lines below.

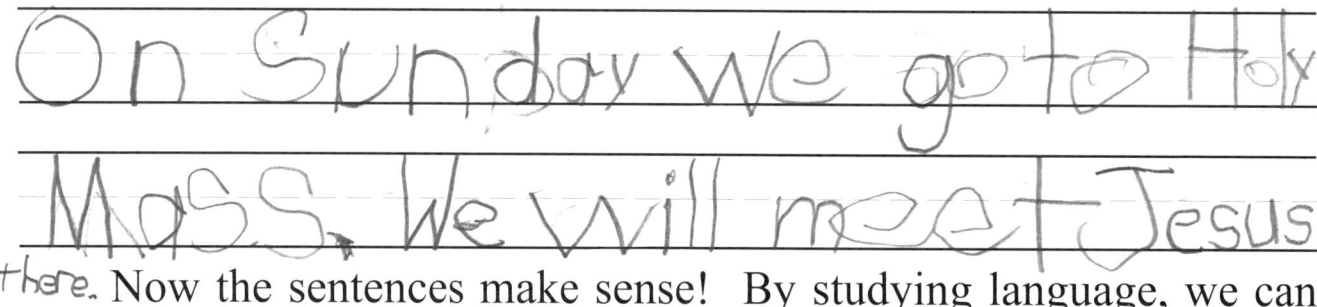

Now the sentences make sense! By studying language, we can learn to *communicate*, to tell our thoughts and beliefs in a way that others may understand.

The most important message that we can communicate is Jesus' loving plan for our lives. In Matthew 28:19–20, Jesus tells us to teach others about Him. To do this, we must first know Him. We must listen to His voice, which we hear through His Holy Catholic Church. The lessons in this book will help you to communicate what you hear and know, to tell the Good News of Jesus.

The Period and Telling Sentences

A sentence tells a complete idea. Telling sentences, or *statements*, end with a period. Read the sentences below. Without periods, is it easy to tell where one sentence ends and the next sentence begins?

God is my Father. Baptism has made me His child. I am part of the family of God. The people in my parish belong to the same family of God. The Church all around the world is part of the same family. God is a loving Father to all His children around the world.

Sentences without periods are hard to understand. Go back to the words in the box and put a period at the end of each sentence. Now read the sentences. They are much easier to understand, aren't they?

A. Put a period at the end of these telling sentences.

1. Jesus sent His followers to teach the world about Him.

2. The Holy Spirit took St. Philip into the desert.

3. There St. Philip met a man from Africa.

4. The man wanted to know more about God.

5. He wanted to be part of God's family.

6. St. Philip told him how to become God's child.

7. There in the desert, they came upon a small pool of water.

8. How happy the man was to be baptized there by St. Philip.

Sentence Parts

A sentence is made of parts that together tell a complete idea.

| kneels | This is not a complete idea. Who or what is kneeling?

| in front of the tabernacle | This is not a complete idea.

| kneels in front of the tabernacle | This is not a complete idea.

Now we know that something or someone is kneeling in front of the tabernacle, but we still don't know who. Let's try one more time.

| The pope kneels in front of the tabernacle. |

Now the sentence is complete. A sentence is made of parts that together tell a complete idea.

A. **Match the sentence parts to make a complete sentence. Make a line to connect the matching parts.**

Part #1
God made

Chocolate ice cream

Mittens make

Last summer, my family

Part #2
tastes good.

me to know Him, love Him and serve Him.

camped in the mountains.

my hands feel toasty.

More Sentence Parts

A sentence is made of parts that together tell a complete idea.
A telling sentence ends with a period.

**A. Print 'C' in the space if the sentence tells a complete idea.
Then put a period at the end of the sentence.
Print 'N' in the space if the parts do not make a complete idea.**

1. __C__ I can love God.

2. ____ can love

3. ____ serve God

4. ____ St. Dominic loved and served God

5. ____ St. Dominic sold his books

6. ____ to feed the poor

7. ____ gave him the rosary

8. ____ the Blessed Mother

9. ____ Our Lady helped St. Dominic to preach

10. ____ whispered in his ear

11. ____ I will ask the Blessed Mother to help me, too

St. Dominic

Complete Sentences

**A sentence is made of parts that together tell a complete idea.
A complete sentence tells the whole idea.**

**A. Print 'C' in the space if the sentence tells a complete idea.
Then put a period at the end of the sentence.
Print 'N' in the space if the parts do not make a complete idea.**

1. ____ the Sacrament of Penance

2. ____ This Sacrament always comes before First Holy Communion

3. ____ know our sins

4. ____ sorry for our sins

5. ____ This Holy Sacrament

6. ____ makes our souls clean

7. ____ pure and spotless

8. ____ Our souls will become pure and spotless

9. ____ Jesus will come to live inside us

10. ____ We will be like beautiful tabernacles

11. ____ joyful day

More Complete Sentences

When we speak and write, we want to choose words, ideas, and sentences that will please God.

A. Pick the sentence parts that will please God. Put the parts together, then print the sentence on the lines.

1. My little brother   is a monster.
             is made in the image of God.

2. It pleases God when I   think of others.
             put myself first.

3. Our Blessed Mother   never paid attention.
             listened to God.

4. I can help to   pick up the toys.
 It's not my turn to

5. I want to   stay in bed.
             be ready for Holy Mass.

Sentences Start with a Capital Letter

**A sentence is made of parts that together tell a complete idea.
A sentence always begins with a capital letter.**

A. Circle the letters that need capitals. Print a capital letter above the circle.

1. (L)ong ago a little boy studied in the country of Ireland.

2. we now know him as Saint Columban.

3. when he was grown, God called him to teach in many far countries.

4. he and his monks started more than one hundred monasteries.

5. there the monks sang praise to Our Lord all day and all night.

6. at times, St. Columban lived in a cave in the mountains.

7. once, when he found a bear in his cave, he told it to leave.

8. the bear quietly obeyed him.

9. much of St. Columban's time was spent in study and writing.

10. he loved the Church and wrote "Rome is the head of the whole world."

11. the Church honors St. Columban on November 23.

Words that Ask

Asking words help us to learn more about people, places, and ideas.

| who   what   when   where   why   how |

Asking words are often used to begin asking sentences. An asking sentence is called a question and always ends with a question mark.

A. **Circle the asking word at the beginning of the question. Then make a question mark at the end of the sentence.**

1. (Why) did God make me ?

2. When will we see His face

3. How can I get to Heaven

4. Who will show me the way

5. Who did God's will in every way

6. Who lived a holy and sinless life

7. Who obeyed God best

8. What does Our Lady say about obeying God

9. Who said, "Let it be done to me according to Your Word"

10. Who said, "Do whatever He tells you"

11. How can I be like Our Lady

12. What would most please Jesus and Mary

Asking and Telling Sentences

Questions often begin with the words *who, what, when, where, why,* and *how.* However, sometimes these words can be used in telling sentences. Many other words can ask questions, too. Read the sentences carefully to see if the words are telling or asking.

A. Some of these sentences are asking sentences. Some of them are telling sentences. Put a question mark at the end of the asking sentences. Put a period at the end of the telling sentences.

1. Why is it important to be truthful

2. Should we always tell the truth

3. Have you ever been hurt by a lie

4. Does God want us to hurt others

5. God loves us and wants us to love each other

6. When we tell the truth, we please God

7. Is it sometimes hard to do what we should

8. If we ask Him, Jesus will help us to do what is right

9. Jesus said, "I am the Way, the Truth, and the Life"

10. Since God made us, doesn't He know what is best for us

11. In the end, we are happiest when we do things God's way

Mixed Sentence Practice

A. **Some of these sentences are asking sentences. Some of them are telling sentences. Put a question mark at the end of the asking sentences. Put a period at the end of the telling sentences.**

1. Josh has just moved into the house down the street

2. Tess and her little brother Greg see Josh walking slowly toward them

3. Greg thinks that Josh walks in a funny way

4. Should Tess and Greg hide in the bushes when Josh comes to play

5. They pretend that they are not at home

6. Is this like telling a lie

7. How do you think this makes Josh feel

8. At home, Mother told Tess and Greg that Josh's legs do not work as well as their legs work

9. She told them that Josh had come to invite them to a party

10. Josh's legs don't work well, but his heart is big and kind

11. What do you think Tess and Greg should do now

Write an ending to this story that would be pleasing to God.

Sentences that Command

Telling sentences are called *statements*, and end with a period. Asking sentences are called *questions*, and end with a question mark. *Commanding* sentences tell you to do something. Commanding sentences also end with a period. When you use commanding sentences, it is often polite to begin with *Please*.

Get my basketball.   Please get my basketball.

Both are commands, but which one is more polite? How do you think the Child Jesus might have spoken to His Mother? The Holy Family's speech was cheerful and polite. Our speech can bring cheer and happiness to our homes, too.

A. **Put a 'C' in the blank if the sentence is a command, a 'T' for telling sentences, and a 'Q' for questions. Then put the correct mark at the end of each sentence.**

____ 1. Mom, I can help clean the fishbowl

____ 2. Please feed the goldfish

____ 3. Where is the baby

____ 4. Please get the baby

____ 5. Wipe his hands well

____ 6. Please find the rest of the goldfish

____ 7. Did you check the baby's pockets

Mixed Sentences

A. Put a 'C' in the blank if the sentence is a command. Put a 'T' in the blank if it is a telling sentence. Put a 'Q' in the blank if it is a question. Then put the correct mark at the end of each sentence.

_____ 1. We will have a party for Grandpa and Grandma

_____ 2. Please help set the table

_____ 3. Have Grandpa and Grandma really been married for fifty years

_____ 4. John, get the fancy blue napkins from the drawer

_____ 5. Grandma and Grandpa like the color blue

_____ 6. The color blue reminds us of the Blessed Mother

_____ 7. Angela, bring me the tablecloth

_____ 8. Please set the cake in the middle of the table

_____ 9. Where are the candles

_____ 10. Put the candles on the cake

_____ 11. Is that the doorbell

_____ 12. Marie, please open the door

_____ 13. Father Paul has come to share the happy day

_____ 14. He will give a special blessing to Grandma and Grandpa

Can and May

Can means that I am able to do something.

I *can* print my name. I *can* run fast.

May is used to ask or show permission.

Please *may* I have a cookie? Yes, you *may* have a cookie.

can	may

A. Choose the correct word to print on the line.

1. I _____ stand on my hands.

2. _____ you jump rope?

3. Dad, please _____ I go to the pool?

4. Yes, you _____ go to the pool.

5. Please _____ I use your rollerblades?

6. _____ we fly our kites in the field?

7. I _____ do seventy jumping jacks.

8. You _____ go outside when you finish your schoolwork.

9. I _____ finish my homework quickly.

10. _____ we watch the Don Bosco movie?

11. Yes, you _____ watch the movie after dinner.

Exclaiming Sentences

You have learned about statements, questions, and commands. Commands tell us to do something. *Exclaiming* sentences show surprise or strong feelings of sadness, fear, or joy.

Christmas is coming!   I hear sirens!

Exclaiming sentences end with an exclamation mark !

A. **Put a 'C' in the blank if the sentence is a command. Put an 'E' in the blank if the sentence is an exclamation. Then put the correct mark at the end of each sentence.** Hint: think of how you might say the sentence if you were the speaker.

_____ 1. Look into the sky

_____ 2. The sun is spinning

_____ 3. Our Lady is here

_____ 4. Listen to her

_____ 5. Pray the Rosary every day

_____ 6. Our Lord and Savior is born

_____ 7. Glory to God

_____ 8. Please help Anna with the dishes

_____ 9. Don't forget to wipe the table

_____ 10. What a big help you are

Photocopying of these pages is strictly illegal and a violation of copyright law.

Mixed Sentence Review

A. Circle 'C' for commanding sentences. Circle 'Q' for questions. Circle 'T' for telling sentences. Circle 'E' for exclamations. Then put the correct mark at the end of each sentence. Hint: think of how you might say the sentence.

C Q T E   1. Go to the upper room

C Q T E   2. There you will find the apostles in prayer

C Q T E   3. You will find Our Blessed Mother with them

C Q T E   4. Are they waiting for Someone

C Q T E   5. I see flames of fire

C Q T E   6. The Holy Spirit has come

C Q T E   7. God be praised

C Q T E   8. What a huge crowd of people

C Q T E   9. Stand here

C Q T E   10. Who is speaking to the crowd

C Q T E   11. Listen to St. Peter

C Q T E   12. Jesus chose him to lead the Church

C Q T E   13. Jesus promised to stay with His Church always

C Q T E   14. God is so faithful

Let's Review

A. **A sentence is made of parts that together tell a complete idea. Match the sentence parts to make a complete sentence. Make a line to connect the matching parts.**

Part #1	Part #2
School often	fall from the trees.
Autumn leaves	begin to fly south for the winter.
Honking geese	shows God's beautiful handiwork.
Each season	starts in September.

B. **Circle the letters that need capitals. Print a capital letter above the circle. Then put the correct mark at the end of the sentence.**

1. which is your favorite season

2. do you like to make snowmen

3. maybe you live in a place that never has snow

4. children in Florida visit the sunny beaches even in December

5. sunshine or snow, December reminds us all of Jesus' birth

6. What do you like to do in the wintertime? Print your answer below.

A Growing Vocabulary: Synonyms

You may know that *vocabulary* means all the words in a language. Your own vocabulary is all the words that *you* know. Learning new words makes it easier for you to understand what you read and hear. A bigger vocabulary will also help you to learn more about our dear Lord. Let us glorify God in our speech and writing.

Synonyms are words that mean almost the same thing. Some words tell our meaning more clearly than others. We may say that our Blessed Mother is *good*. That is true, but ice cream is good, too. Our meaning becomes more clear if we say that our Blessed Mother is *holy.* Holiness is a very special kind of goodness. If we wanted to write about our Blessed Mother, *holy* would be a better word to use.

Synonyms: cold   icy   chilly

Circle the synonym.

smell	look	eat	(sniff)	blow
touch	like	smell	hand	stroke
jump	walk	leap	run	sniff
walk	outside	hike	camp	shoe
glorify	praise	good	sing	hike
know	have	believe	prayer	true
sure	not	maybe	certain	have

More Synonyms

finished   shut   present

adore   silently

A. Print the synonym in the blank.

1. The altar boys enter [quietly] **silently**.

2. At Holy Mass, Our Lord is [here]_____ on the altar.

3. Even the angels bow to [worship]_____ Him.

4. I [close]_____ my eyes and tell Jesus that I love Him.

5. When Holy Mass is [done]_____, I thank Jesus with a full heart.

---
believe   raised   positive   loving

B. Print the synonym in the blank.

Once, a priest was not [sure]_____ that Jesus was truly present on the altar. As he [lifted]_____ the Host, the priest saw that it truly became the flesh of Jesus. We do not need to see the Host change to [know]_____ that Jesus is truly present. We know that it is true, because Jesus told us so. How [caring]_____ God is, to come down from Heaven to make His home inside us.

Photocopying of these pages is strictly illegal and a violation of copyright law.

Fun with Synonyms

A. Print the synonym on the line.

| crib |
| infant |
| snoozing |

1. The baby is [sleeping]_____ in his bed.

2. The [baby]_____ is snoozing in his bed.

3. The infant is snoozing in his [bed]_____.

Which sentence below sounds more interesting?

The baby is sleeping in his bed. OR The infant is snoozing in his crib.

B. Choose a different synonym for each circled word. Then print the new sentence on the lines below.

See the (dog)   (run) through the grassy (field.)

pup	race	meadow
mongrel	scamper	clearing
pooch	flee	pasture

_____
_____
_____
_____

Turn to Appendix for writing exercises.

A Growing Vocabulary: Antonyms

"...once you were darkness, but now you are light in the Lord..."
Eph. 5:8

Holy Scripture sometimes uses the words 'dark' and 'darkness' to speak of what is evil. The opposite of evil is goodness. Because the opposite of 'dark' is 'light,' Holy Scripture often uses the word 'light' to tell about God and goodness. Words that are opposites are called *antonyms*.

"For with thee is the fountain of life; and in thy light we shall see light."
Psalm 35:10, Douay Rheims

Circle the antonym.

clean	washed	dirty	soap	dry
give	gift	spend	take	buy
joy	happy	frown	smile	sorrow
find	drop	lose	give	see
late	bed	arrive	early	time
asleep	awake	snooze	up	bed
evil	sin	good	bad	sorry
wise	sad	smart	foolish	happy

Turn to Appendix for writing exercises.

Photocopying of these pages is strictly illegal and a violation of copyright law.

More Antonyms

| excited   whispers   early   older   carefully |

A. Print the correct antonym on the line.

1. John wants to be a priest when he is [younger] _____.

2. He gets up [late] _____ to be ready for Holy Mass.

3. Father quietly [yells] _____ directions to John.

4. John listens [carelessly] _____ to Father's words.

5. John is [bored] _____ and happy to serve at Jesus' altar.

B. Match the opposites.

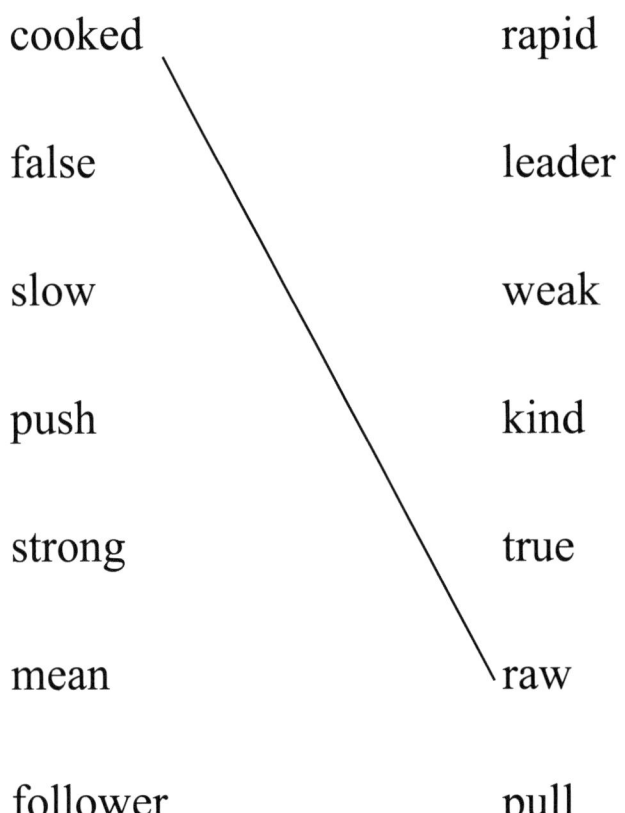

cooked   rapid

false   leader

slow   weak

push   kind

strong   true

mean   raw

follower   pull

I will go unto the altar of God: unto God who gives joy to my youth.

Homophones

Some words, called *homophones* or *homonyms*, sound the same but have different spellings and meanings.

Son   **sun**

A. Underline the correct homophone.

1. Our Lord Jesus Christ is God the [Son sun].

2. Mary is always ready to [hear here] God's word.

3. I want to [bee be] like Mary.

4. She is my [dear deer] Mother.

B. Match the homophone to its definition.

brakes	damages or destroys
breaks	used to stop a bike or car
weak	a seven-day period
week	not strong
pear	a tasty fruit
pair	a group of two things
see	ocean
sea	look

Nouns

Words that name people, places, or things are called *nouns*. Most nouns are things that you can touch. You can touch a flower. You can touch a hat. *Flower* and *hat* are nouns.

[policeman]
person

[the mountains]
place

[hat]
thing

A. **Circle the words that name a person, place, or thing.**

flower	ran	blue
under	wet	sock
down	girl	blue
house	tried	safely
brown	ate	helmet
careful	rollerblades	fast
loving	grandma	rocking
popsicle	lick	chilly

Nouns in Sentences

A. Ask: is this a person, place, or thing? Then circle the nouns in the sentences.

1. A (child) is waiting for the (priest).
2. The boy will go into the peaceful confessional.
3. Perhaps he will use a kneeler made of wood.
4. Maybe he will sit on a chair under a crucifix.
5. The boy will tell Jesus that he is sorry.
6. It is God Himself who forgives.
7. This happy young man will be skipping back to his house.

B. Ask: is this a person, place, or thing? Then circle the nouns in the sentences.

8. Hundreds and hundreds of families sat on the hillside, listening to Jesus.
9. Mothers watched their small children playing in the warm grass.
10. Soon little stomachs began to growl and babies began to cry.
11. The people wanted lunch, but there was no food to eat.
12. Then a little boy gave Jesus his small basket of fish and rolls.
13. Jesus looked up to heaven and blessed the food.
14. He broke the bread in His hands and made it grow and grow.
15. Jesus fed all the hungry men, women, and children.
16. Now Jesus feeds people all over the world with His living Bread.

Photocopying of these pages is strictly illegal and a violation of copyright law.

Proper Nouns

Words that name people, places, or things are called *nouns*. *Common nouns* name any person, place, or thing. *Proper nouns* name a *specific* person, place, or thing. Because proper nouns are names, they are always capitalized. *If two words make up the proper noun, both are capitalized.*

common noun=any police officer
specific officer=Officer Robert
Officer Robert=proper noun

common noun=any mountains
specific mountains=Rocky Mountains
Rocky Mountains=proper noun

common noun=any aunt
specific aunt=Aunt Rita
Aunt Rita=proper noun

common noun=any sister
specific sister=Sister Lucia
Sister Lucia=proper noun

A. Circle the *proper nouns* that name a specific person, place, or thing. Put an X on the common nouns.

~~boy~~	(Dan)	blue
Uncle Rick	uncle	hat
land	Boston	city
Father Karl	priest	father
church	Holy Name Church	pray
water	Red River	river

More Proper Nouns

A. | Proper nouns can name people. Proper nouns are capitalized. |

Your name is a proper noun. Print it here:_____

The name of your bishop is also a proper noun.

Print his name here:_____

| Proper nouns can name places. Proper nouns are capitalized. |

Print the name of your street or road here:_____

Print the name of your city here:_____

Print the name of your state:_____

Print the name of a nearby lake or river:_____

Print the name of your parish:_____

B. Find the proper nouns in these sentences. Circle the words that need capitals. Then print the capital above the circle. Underline common nouns.

1. (nathan) (marie) and their <u>parents</u> flew to (rome.)
   [N above nathan, M above marie, R above rome]

2. Their car took them past beautiful churches and over the tiber river.

3. The city was filled with statues of many popes and saints.

4. The family was able to see pope francis at saint peter's church.

Photocopying of these pages is strictly illegal and a violation of copyright law.

Capital Letters and God's Name

Names begin with capital letters. There are many different 'names' or *titles* for God, such as 'Lord' and 'Savior.' No matter which name or title is used, God's Name always begins with a capital letter.

A. Print the missing capital letters to finish spelling titles for God.

Redeemer

Father

Son

Holy Spirit

Lord

Holy Trinity

Jesus Christ

Good Shepherd

___esus ___hrist

___ord

___ather

___ood ___hepherd

___edeemer

___oly ___pirit

___on

___oly ___rinity

B. Circle the letters that need capitals. Print the capital letter above the circle.

1. jesus christ is my lord, savior, and redeemer.

2. The holy trinity is god the father, god the son, and god the holy spirit.

3. With the son and holy spirit, god the father created all things.

God's Name and Other Titles

There are many different *titles* for God. There are also special titles for Our Lady. These names and titles always begins with capital letters. [Just for fun, see how many different titles you can find in your prayer book.]

A. Print the missing capital letters to finish spelling titles for God and for Our Lady.

God

| Body of Christ |
| King of Kings |
| Sacred Heart |
| Lamb of God |
| Blessed Sacrament |

___acred ___eart

___ing of ___ings

___lessed ___acrament

___ody of ___hrist

___amb of ___od

Mary

| Blessed Virgin |
| Blessed Mother |
| Mystical Rose |
| Mother of God |

___ystical ___ose

___lessed ___other

___other of ___od

___lessed ___irgin

B. Circle the letters that need capitals. Print the capital letter above the circle.

1. mary is called the mother of god, because her son, jesus, is god the son.

2. The blessed sacrament is truly the body of christ.

Let's Review

A. Circle the synonym.

look	eat	view	sniff	blow
make	like	create	hand	paint
fix	break	leap	run	repair

B. Circle the antonym.

fix	repair	eat	break	blow
make	create	destroy	hand	stroke
cloudy	sunny	hot	run	rainy

C. Circle the correct homophone.

son   sun

pear   pair

D. Print 'C' if the sentence is complete. Print 'N' if the sentence is not complete.

1. ____ went hiking yesterday.

2. ____ Yesterday we hiked to Deer Lake.

3. ____ Later in the day

4. ____ a meadow covered with wild yellow daisies.

5. ____ We praised God for the majesty of His creation.

Turn to Appendix for writing exercises.

More Review

A. Circle 'C' for commanding sentences. Circle 'Q' for questions. Circle 'T' for telling sentences. Circle 'E' for exclamations. Then put the correct mark at the end of each sentence.

C Q T E   1. Can you climb to the top of the tree

C Q T E   2. Hold on tightly

C Q T E   3. I'm slipping

C Q T E   4. Are you hurt

C Q T E   5. No, I didn't even get a scratch

B. Print 'P' for proper nouns. Print 'C' for common nouns.

1. ____ river   5. ____ Colorado River

2. ____ Father Charles   6. ____ Saint Michael's Church

3. ____ priest   7. ____ dog

4. ____ road   8. ____ Main Street

C. Circle the letters that need capitals. Print the capital letter above the circle.

1. i believe in the holy trinity: father, son, and holy spirit.

2. mary is the mother of god and my blessed mother, too.

3. jesus is the lamb of god who was sacrificed on calvary.

Turn to Appendix for writing exercises.

One and More Than One

Sometimes when we have one thing, we call it a **single** thing.

one rabbit= one single rabbit

In writing, a word that tells about one thing is called **singular**. A word that tells about a group of things is called **plural**. To make a word plural, add an 's' at the end of the word.

singular: rabbit   **plural:** rabbits

A. Print the word. Add 's' at the end to make it plural.

Singular	Plural	Singular	Plural
tree	**trees**	rock	_____
key	_____	fork	_____

Words that end with *ch, sh, ss, s, x,* and *z* add the suffix 'es' to make plurals.

B. Print the word. Add 'es' to make it plural.

dress _____   match _____

dish _____   fox _____

glass _____   branch _____

Mixed Plurals

A. Print the noun. Remember the rule, adding 'es' or 's' to make plural nouns.

Singular	Plural		Singular	Plural
1. truck	_____		11. paper	_____
2. beach	_____		12. branch	_____
3. class	_____		13. patch	_____
4. dish	_____		14. bird	_____
5. desk	_____		15. cake	_____
6. carrot	_____		16. letter	_____
7. dress	_____		17. squash	_____
8. shirt	_____			
9. chair	_____			
10. fox	_____			

We give Thee thanks, O Lord, for the gifts that we receive from Thy grace and bounty.

Consonant +y Plurals

When a word ends in consonant +y, make a plural by changing the 'y' to 'i' and adding 'es.'

A. Make these nouns plural by changing the 'y' to 'i' and adding 'es.'

Singular	Plural	Singular	Plural
copy	copies	puppy	
cherry		penny	
sky		berry	

Most plurals are made by adding 's' or 'es.' Some words follow a different pattern. A few words are used for both singular and plural.

B. Match these words with their plurals.

man	sheep
woman	feet
goose	children
foot	women
sheep	geese
tooth	men
deer	teeth
child	deer

Plural Practice

A. Circle the word with the correct plural ending. Remember that nouns ending in *ch, sh, ss, s, x,* and *z* add 'es' to make a plural ending.

medal	medales	medalz	medals
font	fontes	fontz	fonts
bush	bushs	bushes	bushz
church	churchz	churchs	churches
woman	wommin	womens	women
crutch	crutches	crutchs	crutchis
rosary	rosaries	rosarys	rosarees
watch	watchs	watchies	watches
stamp	stampes	stamps	stamp
deer	deers	deeres	deer
goose	gooses	geese	goose
foot	foots	feets	feet
puppy	puppys	puppies	puppyes
brush	brushiz	brushes	brushs

Photocopying of these pages is strictly illegal and a violation of copyright law.

Possessive Nouns

Mike's bike

An 's' added to the end of a noun does not always make the word a plural.

This mark— ' —is called an *apostrophe*. An apostrophe and the letter 's' together show possession or ownership.

A. **Add apostrophe + s to show possession.**

Rachel___ skirt   Jose____ prayer book

dog___ breath   Rita___ sweater

boys

boy's drum

In the first picture are two boys, plural. No apostrophe +s is used. In the second picture, one boy has possession of a drum. We use apostrophe +s to show possession.

B. **Print 'PLU' in the blank if the word is plural. Print 'POS' if the word shows possession.**

1. _____ David's glove   4. _____ dogs barking

2. _____ holy angels   5. _____ angel's wing

3. _____ Dana's cup   6. _____ cups

Finding Possessives

A. **Circle possessive nouns.**
Put an X over plural nouns.

King Darius had a wicked advisor who was jealous of Daniel. He was jealous of (Daniel's) wisdom. He and his nasty ~~partners~~ were also jealous of Daniel's friendship with the king.

This wicked advisor tricked the ruler into signing an order to trap Daniel. The king's order said that no one could pray to anyone but to him. Anyone who did not obey the king's decree would be thrown into a den of mean, hungry lions.

However, Daniel was God's servant. His prayers would be to God alone. One day, Daniel was faithfully praying inside his house. Daniel's window was wide open, so all who passed by could see Daniel praying.

Sadly, the advisor's plan worked. Daniel was caught, arrested, and cruelly tossed into the den of lions. A huge stone was rolled in front of the den's opening, making escape impossible. As a roaring lion walked toward Daniel, Our Lord slammed the lion's mouth shut. God was keeping Daniel safe even in the midst of wild beasts.

Meanwhile, King Darius, who was really Daniel's friend, also cried out to God to spare Daniel's life. Hours later, when the king saw that Daniel was still alive, he ordered that Daniel be pulled out of the den.

King Darius saw that neither were Daniel's bones broken nor did he have any scratches on him, so he wrote a new order. The ruler's new decree was to all peoples and nations. It commanded worship of the true God, who has worked signs and wonders in heaven and on earth, and who saved Daniel from the jaws of lions.

Photocopying of these pages is strictly illegal and a violation of copyright law.

Mixed Plurals and Possessives

A. Circle the correct word.

1. Two [trees tree's] blew down in the windstorm.

2. That [trees tree's] leaves are falling quietly on our lawn.

3. Did you see the bright angels on the [books book's] cover?

4. Let's check out some [books book's] about the Little Flower.

5. Have you seen [Jesses Jesse's] prayer book?

6. Erin cheerfully put away her dresses and [skirts skirt's].

7. Mom, could you please sew the tear in my [skirts skirt's] hem?

8. The crowd threw [stones stone's] at St. Stephen.

9. [St. Stephens St. Stephen's] face glowed with heavenly light.

B. Print 'PLU' in the blank if the underlined word is plural. Print 'POS' if the word shows possession.

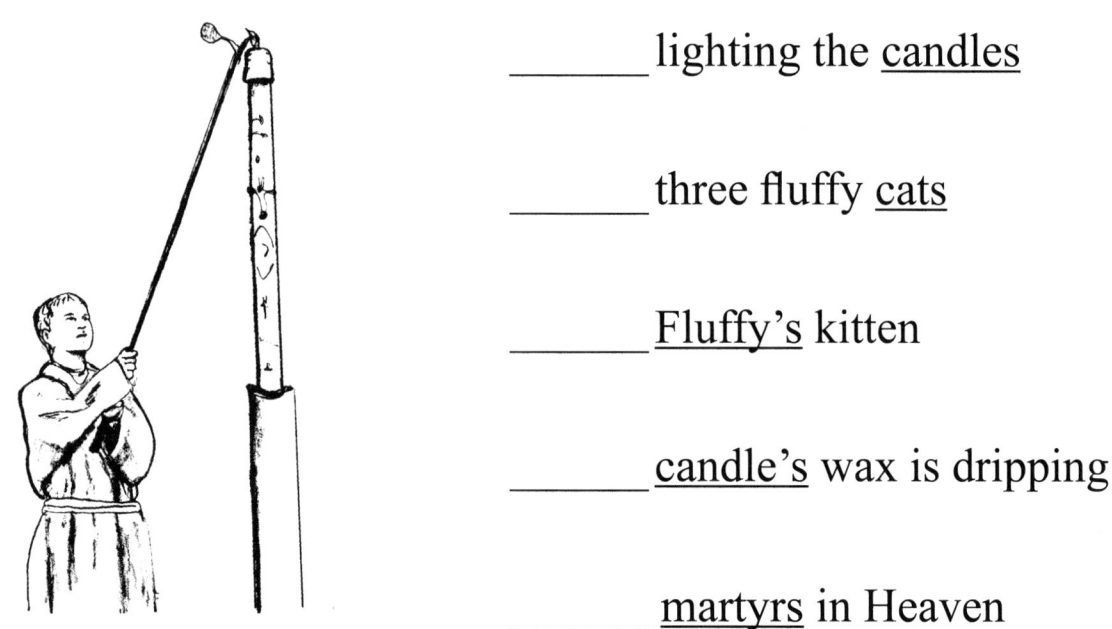

_____ lighting the <u>candles</u>

_____ three fluffy <u>cats</u>

_____ <u>Fluffy's</u> kitten

_____ <u>candle's</u> wax is dripping

_____ <u>martyrs</u> in Heaven

Action Words

Verbs are action words that tell about something that you can **do**. Remember that most nouns are things that you can touch. Verbs are things that you can do. Can you touch *climb* or *throw*? No, climb and throw are things that you do, not things that you can touch. *Climb* and *throw* are action words. They are verbs.

climb

throw

A. Circle the action words.

1.	paper	run	rug
2.	hop	wet	frog
3.	sidewalk	girl	jumping
4.	sing	altar	church
5.	hit	silly	chair
6.	Mass	prayer book	pray
7.	push	cart	hill
8.	bubbles	blowing	bottle

More Action Words

Verbs are action words that tell about something that you can **do**.

A. Pick a word from the box. Print it on the line under the correct picture.

_____   _____   _____

B. Cross out all the words that are NOT action words.

1.	tiptoe	~~flower~~	~~plate~~
2.	chalk	skip	sidewalk
3.	splash	fins	pool
4.	blanket	bed	sleep
5.	crucifix	pray	church
6.	pecking	birdfeeder	robin
7.	milk	glass	sip
8.	scrub	sink	towel

Turn to Appendix for writing exercises.

State of Being Verbs

The verbs *am*, *is,* and *are* do not show action, but *state of being*. For example, can you clap? Yes. *Clap* is something that you can do. It is an action. Can you short? No, *short* is not an action. Can you hungry? No, *hungry* is not an action. But you can *be* short. You can *be* hungry. Short and hungry tell about *states of being*.

Jose <u>is</u> smart.   I <u>am</u> short.   The boys <u>are</u> hungry.

A. Pick a word from the box to tell about state of being. Print the correct word in the sentences below.

| am | is | are |

1. It _____ wintertime.

2. My fingers _____ cold.

3. Matt's pony _____ fast.

4. The saddle _____ squeaky.

5. I _____ a cowboy.

6. God _____ love.

7. My Guardian Angel _____ powerful.

8. I _____ not afraid because the Blessed Mother watches me, too.

9. With so many heavenly friends, we _____ never alone.

Turn to Appendix for writing exercises.

Photocopying of these pages is strictly illegal and a violation of copyright law.

State of Being: Present Tense

The verbs *am*, *is,* and *are* tell about now, or the *present.* They do not show action, but *state of being.* Because God has no beginning and no end, He IS. God is always in the present.

A. Pick a word from the box to tell about state of being. Print the correct word in the sentences below.

| am | is | are |

1. God _____ all-mighty.

2. I _____ a good reader.

3. God _____ my Father.

4. I _____ God's child.

5. Vincent's tie _____ tight.

6. His shoes _____ new.

7. Holy Scripture _____ God's word.

8. God _____ all-wise.

9. Jesus' teachings _____ true.

10. Angels _____ spirits.

11. I _____ a Catholic.

Photocopying of these pages is strictly illegal and a violation of copyright law.

Action and State of Being Verbs

The verbs *am, is,* and *are* tell about now, or the *present*. They do not show action, but *state of being*.

A. If the verb shows action, print 'act' in the blank. If the verb shows state of being, print 'be.' Verbs are underlined.

1. _____ I <u>am</u> eight years old.

2. _____ It <u>is</u> a rainy day.

3. _____ We <u>are</u> in the parish hall.

4. _____ Our class <u>studies</u> about Jesus in the Blessed Sacrament.

5. _____ Vincent <u>wears</u> his best suit and tie.

6. _____ I <u>am</u> happy.

7. _____ We <u>walk</u> to the front of the church.

8. _____ Lupe <u>kneels</u> at the altar rail.

9. _____ The priest <u>is</u> kind.

10. _____ The church <u>is</u> quiet.

11. _____ My Jesus <u>comes</u> to me in Holy Communion.

12. _____ Our hearts <u>are</u> full.

13. _____ Lupe <u>lays</u> the flowers next to the tabernacle.

14. _____ My parents <u>hug</u> me.

Photocopying of these pages is strictly illegal and a violation of copyright law.

More Action and State of Being Verbs

A. **Find and circle the verb in each sentence. If the word shows action, print 'act' in the blank. If the word shows state of being, print 'be.'**

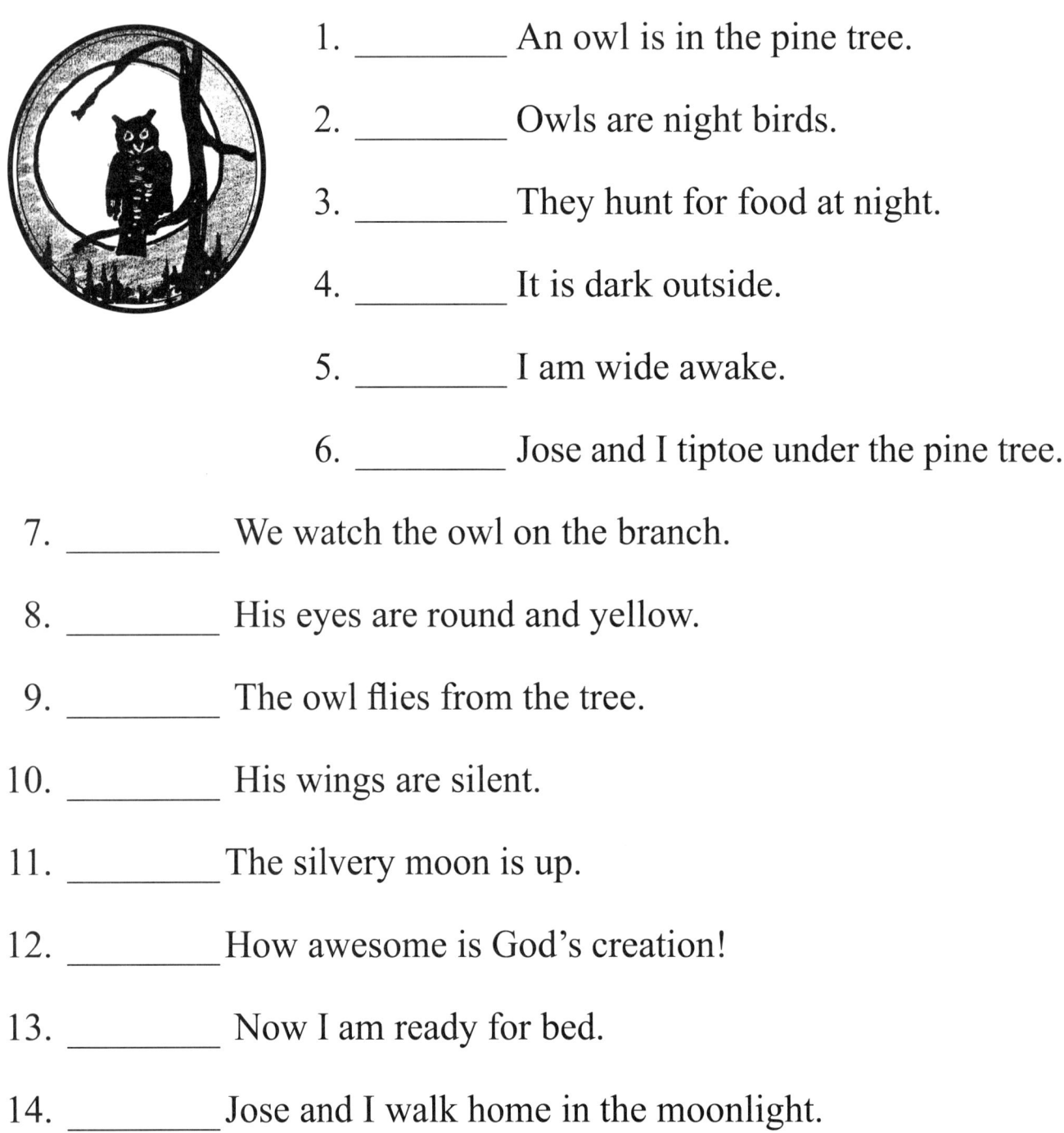

1. _____ An owl is in the pine tree.
2. _____ Owls are night birds.
3. _____ They hunt for food at night.
4. _____ It is dark outside.
5. _____ I am wide awake.
6. _____ Jose and I tiptoe under the pine tree.
7. _____ We watch the owl on the branch.
8. _____ His eyes are round and yellow.
9. _____ The owl flies from the tree.
10. _____ His wings are silent.
11. _____ The silvery moon is up.
12. _____ How awesome is God's creation!
13. _____ Now I am ready for bed.
14. _____ Jose and I walk home in the moonlight.

State of Being: Present and Past Tense

The verbs *am, is,* and *are* tell about now, or the *present*. They are present tense verbs.

A. Find and circle the verbs that tell about now. Print 'now' on the line.

1. _____ Children are at the beach.

2. _____ The weather is sunny.

3. _____ I am sandy.

The words *was* and *were* are state of being verbs that tell about the *past*. They can tell about long ago, a few minutes ago, or any time that is in the past. *Was* tells about one thing. *Were* tells about more than one. *Was* and *were* are *past tense* verbs.

B. Pick a word from the box to tell about the past. Print the correct word in the sentences below.

was	were

1. Yesterday, I _____ outside.

2. Yesterday, the weather _____ sunny.

3. Yesterday, children _____ at the beach.

4. Last week, Dad _____ busy.

5. A year ago, these sleeves _____ too long.

More Present and Past Tense Verbs

The verbs *am, is,* and *are* tell about the *present.* The verbs *was* and *were* are state of being verbs that tell about the *past*.

A. Underline the verb. If the verb is present tense, print 'present' in the blank. If the verb is past tense, print 'past' in the blank.

1. _____ Last year, I was eight years old.

2. _____ Now I am nine years old.

3. _____ Mark and Joseph are my little brothers.

4. _____ This morning, they were under the bed.

5. _____ It is dusty under the bed.

6. _____ Now the boys are in the bathtub.

7. _____ A pile of leaves was in Mrs. Garcia's yard.

8. _____ The leaves were soggy.

9. _____ Our rake was heavy.

10. _____ My boots were slippery.

11. _____ My jeans were wet and dirty.

12. _____ The leaves are not there today.

13. _____ Mrs. Garcia is grateful.

Helping Verbs

The verbs *am*, *is,* and *are* tell about the *present*. The verbs *was* and *were* tell about the *past*. These state of being verbs also can do another job as *helping verbs*. *Helping verbs* work together with action verbs to tell more about what is happening or has happened.

I <u>am</u> in the pool.   **am=being verb**
I <u>splash</u> in the pool.   **splash=action verb**

Am is a state of being verb. *Splash* and *splashing* are action verbs. *Am* can work with *splashing* to tell more about something that is happening now.

I <u>am splashing</u> in the pool.   **am=used as helping verb, present tense**
I <u>was splashing</u> in the pool. **was=used as helping verb, past tense**

A. **Pick the correct word from the helping verb box. Pick any word from the action verb box. Print the two words on the line to finish the sentence. Follow the directions to make past tense or present tense.**

Helping Verbs   **Action Verbs**

| am   is   are   was   were | | sleeping   bouncing   sitting   reading |

1. [Past] Yesterday, I_____ _____ in the chair.

2. [Present] Today, I_____ _____ in the chair.

3. [Present] We_____ _____ in the chair.

4. [Past] We_____ _____ in the chair.

Photocopying of these pages is strictly illegal and a violation of copyright law.

More Helping Verbs

Helping verbs work with action verbs to tell more about what is happening or has happened.

helping verbs: am   is   are   was   were

A.   Circle the helping verbs. Underline the verbs that show action.

1. Ramon (was) <u>flying</u> his kite in the field.

2. The wind was blowing his kite high into the blue sky.

3. Swallows were racing past the kite.

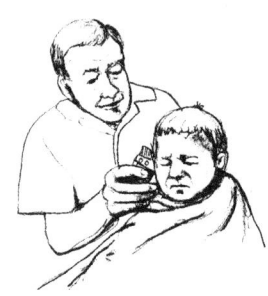

4. The barber is cutting Greg's hair.

5. Greg is wiggling in the barber's chair.

6. Scratchy hairs are falling into his collar.

B.   Underline the verbs. Tell whether they are past or present.

1. __past__   Mother Angelica <u>was talking</u> on TV.

2. _____   Her guests were cheering.

3. _____   The bishop is building a new seminary.

4. _____   Many seminarians are studying there.

5. _____   Our Lady is forming new priests for the Catholic Church.

6. _____   I was taking money out of my piggy bank.

7. _____   I am sending the money to a priest in India.

Let's Review

A. Circle the correct plural form.

1. key	keies	keyes	keys
2. beach	beachies	beaches	beachs
3. cherry	cherries	cherryes	cherrys
4. branch	branchies	branches	branchs
5. medal	medalies	medales	medals
6. kitty	kitties	kittyes	kittys
7. rock	rockies	rockes	rocks
8. guess	guessies	guesses	guessesss
9. fox	foxies	foxes	foxs
10. foot	feet	footes	foots
11. goose	goosies	geese	geeses
12. berry	berries	berryes	berrys

B. Circle the possessive form.

roses and bears   Rose's teddy bear

Noah's ark   animals in the ark

boy's roller blade   boys roller blade

Photocopying of these pages is strictly illegal and a violation of copyright law.

More Review

A. **Circle the action verbs.**

ship	sailing	water
swim	wet	beach
starfish	sand	fishing
cook	fish	Friday
dinner	table	eating
pour	glass	milk

B. **Underline the verbs. Remember helping verbs, too.**

1. St. Paul was sailing on a ship for Rome.

2. Stormy seas were wrecking the ship.

3. People from the ship swam to the beach of a nearby island.

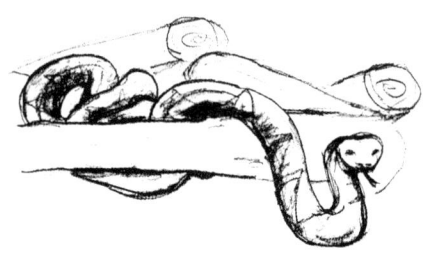

4. A fire was built to dry their clothes.

5. St. Paul threw some wood on the fire.

6. He was bitten by a deadly snake.

7. St. Paul shook the snake into the fire.

8. God was protecting St. Paul.

Turn to Appendix for writing exercises.

Plurals with Verbs

You remember that plural means more than one. When verbs follow plural nouns, something interesting happens to the verb.

one egg:	two or more eggs:
The egg break**s**.	The egg**s** break.

Egg is the noun. *Break* is the action verb.

*If the noun doing the action ends in **-s**, the verb does not end in **-s**.*

A. Circle the correct verb.

1. The girls [**fill** fills] the food basket.
2. The girl [fill fills] the food basket.
3. The boy [carry carries] the boxes.
4. The boys [carry carries] the boxes.
5. Cans [roll rolls] off the table with a bang.
6. A can [roll rolls] off the table with a bang.
7. Mom [jump jumps] at the sudden sound.
8. Rita [cut cuts] the spicy fruitcakes.
9. The Christmas baskets [feed feeds] the poor and hungry.
10. The Christmas basket [feed feeds] the poor and hungry.
11. Jesus [command commands] that we care for the least of these.
12. God [give gives] us many ways to show our love for Him.

Turn to Appendix for writing exercises.

Verbs with Singular and Plural

Action words end in **-s** if the person, place, or thing [noun] doing the action is singular.

Yes: one -s   One <u>boy</u> skat(es).
Yes: one -s   Two <u>bo(ys)</u> skate.
No: two -s   Two <u>bo(ys)</u> skat(es).

In other words, only one of the words will end in **-s**.

A.   Follow the rules for adding -s. Print *yes* on the line if the word needs -s. Print *no* on the line if no -s is needed.

__yes__   1. The <u>boy</u> shovel**s**   deep snowdrifts.

__no__   2. Soft <u>flakes</u> fall   on his cheeks.

_____ 3. The <u>shovel</u> dig   deeply.

_____ 4. Pete's <u>sister</u> place   her shovel on the snow.

_____ 5. <u>Molly</u> lie   down in the sparkling drifts.

_____ 6. Her <u>arms</u> move   up and down in the snow.

_____ 7. <u>Pete</u> see   his sister making a snow angel.

_____ 8. <u>Angels</u> make   him remember the first Christmas.

_____ 9. <u>Stars</u> shine   brightly in the evening sky.

_____ 10. <u>Pete</u> walk   home with his sister thinking of the Infant Jesus.

Have and Has

Has and *have* are present tense verbs. They tell about what happens now. Often, *has* follows a singular noun, and *have* follows plural nouns.

The chicken *has* a nest.   The chickens *have* nests.
The flower *has* petals.   Flowers *have* petals.
My brother *has* a fork.   My brother and sister *have* forks.

Watch out!!
_I_ and _you_ always use _have_, even though they are singular.

You have a fork.   I have a spoon.

A. Print the correct word on the line. | has   have |

1. My parents _____ a shrine for Our Lady in the back yard.

2. The shrine _____ pink roses planted all around it.

3. Matt and I _____ little visits with our Blessed Mother there.

4. The girls _____ ice cream.

5. Matt and Jon _____ ice cream, too.

6. Matt _____ a cone.

7. I _____ two scoops of ice cream in a dish.

More Have and Has

A. Circle the correct verb.

1. Tadpoles [have has] long tails.

2. Adult frogs [have has] webbed feet.

3. My pet frog [have has] a home in a fishbowl.

4. A chicken's egg [have has] a hard shell.

5. Chicks [have has] soft, downy feathers.

6. Hens [have has] wide wings for protecting chicks.

7. That red hen [have has] a chick hiding under her wing.

8. Our Lady [have has] a crown of stars.

9. She [have has] her hands folded in prayer.

10. Mary [have has] the world under her feet.

11. She [have has] two angels at her side.

12. One angel [have has] flowers in its arms.

13. The other angel [have has] a mighty sword.

14. Both angels [have has] their eyes fixed on Our Lady.

15. May all peoples and nations [have has] eyes that are fixed on her.

Past Tense Verbs with -ed

Verbs can tell about past and present. Some action words can be changed to past by adding -ed.

Present
The children *seat* themselves on the floor.
They *listen* to the story.

Past
The children *seated* themselves on the floor.
They *listened* to the story.

A. Add -ed to make the verbs tell about the past.

1. Dad reach for the Holy Bible next to his chair.

2. The children plead_____ to hear the story of Samuel and Eli.

3. Dad carefully open_____ the Holy Scriptures.

4. Samuel was a little boy who help_____ Eli in the temple.

5. One night, a voice call_____ Samuel's name.

6. It was Our Lord who talk_____ to little Samuel.

7. Samuel listen_____ carefully to God's word.

8. Then he hasten_____ to do all that God ask_____ of him.

Verbs that Change Form

Many past tense verbs end in *-ed*. Other verbs change form to become past tense.

Present	Past
Josh *comes* to church.	Josh *came* to church.
Father *speaks* to him.	Father *spoke* to him
Josh *makes* a good confession.	Josh *made* a good confession.

A. Draw lines to match present tense verbs with their past tense forms.

Present	Past
Today we......	Yesterday we.......
sing	ran
eat	drank
sit	wrote
write	saw
sleep	sang
drink	sat
see	slept
run	ate

Have and Has as Helpers

You know that *has* and *have* can tell about the present. *Has* and *have* can also be past tense helping verbs.

The chicken *has laid* an egg in her nest.
The chicks *have run* to the hen.
The chicks *have hidden* under her wings.

A. Circle the helping verbs. Underline the verbs that show action.

1. Jesus (has) prayed all night in the Garden of Gethsemane.

2. All the apostles have slept the night away.

3. Judas has given Our Lord a cruel kiss.

4. How much this kiss has hurt Our Lord!

5. The soldiers have arrested Jesus.

6. Now they have taken him to Pilate.

7. Pilate has washed his hands.

8. Our Lord has lifted the cross to His shoulder.

9. Now He has fallen on the rough stones.

10. Who has cared for Him?

11. Simon of Cyrene has helped with the heavy cross.

12. Veronica has wiped the blood from His face.

13. Our dear Lord has blessed them.

Past Tense Practice

You know that *has* and *have* can tell about both past and present. We can use these words to tell others about God's faithfulness now and in the past. *Had* is a verb that can stand by itself or act as a helping verb. Like *was* and *were*, *had* tells only about the past.

Mary *had* a Baby.
Simeon *had waited* in the temple.
He *had hoped* in God's promise.

A. Circle the helping verbs. Underline the verbs that show action or state of being.

1. Simeon was an old, old man.

2. For many years, he had come to God's house every day.

3. He had hoped in God's promise.

4. How long he had waited!

5. St. Joseph and Mary have travelled to the temple with Baby Jesus.

6. Simeon's eyes opened wide.

7. Our Lady had handed the Child to him.

8. Simeon was praising God.

9. He had found his Infant Savior.

10. We have found the Savior in God's house, too.

More Verbs that Change Form

Many past tense verbs end in *-ed*. Other verbs change form to become past tense. Some forms always take a helping verb.

Present	Past
Today I *go* to church.	Yesterday I *went* to church.
Today Sara *goes* to church.	Yesterday Sara *went* to church.
Today I *do* my chores.	Yesterday I *did* my chores.
Today Sara *does* her chores.	Yesterday Sara *did* her chores.

Some forms always take a helping verb.

gone= past form of go, always takes a helper
done= past form of did, always takes a helper

I *have gone* to church.   Sara *has gone* to church.
I *have done* my chores.   Sara *has done* her chores

A. Print the correct word on the line. Watch for helping verbs.

> go   went   gone   do   did   done

1. Yesterday, I _____ to the park.

2. Sara has _____ to the park, too.

3. Yes, I have _____ the dishes.

4. Now we can _____ to the zoo.

5. I _____ my math last night.

6. Sara has _____ her spelling, too.

7. I can _____ my spelling now, too.

Practice with Verbs and Helping Verbs

Many past tense verbs end in *-ed*. Some verbs change form by adding *-ing*. These verbs can be used for past and present tense.

<u>Present</u>
We *are swimming*.
It *is raining*.

<u>Past</u>
We *were swimming*.
It *was raining*.

*Verbs that end in **-ing** always need a helping verb.*

A. Circle the helping verbs. Underline the verbs that show action. Then tell whether the sentence is past or present.

present 1. David (is) making rosaries.

_____ 2. First, he cuts a long piece of cord.

_____ 3. Beads are sorted in a tray.

_____ 4. He has mailed rosaries to missions in India.

_____ 5. Last year, he made eighty rosaries.

_____ 6. David's sisters have finished one hundred more.

_____ 7. They were praying a 'Hail Mary' on each bead.

_____ 8. Yesterday they went to the post office with another box.

_____ 9. They have done their best for Our Lady.

_____ 10. I am starting some rosaries, too.

Turn to Appendix for writing exercises.

Subjects: One of Two Sentence Parts

A sentence is made of parts that together tell a complete idea. When two or more sentence parts are put together, they make a complete idea, or a complete sentence.

<u>who or what</u>   <u>doing</u>
The chair   is rocking.
David   makes rosaries.

The chair is the <u>who or what</u> part. What is the chair doing? The chair is rocking.

<u>Who</u> makes rosaries? David makes rosaries. The <u>who or what</u> part is called the *subject* of the sentence.

A. Ask <u>who</u> or <u>what</u>. Then underline the subject.

1. <u>An angel</u> spoke to the children at Fatima.

2. The children saw a golden chalice in his hand.

3. The angel held a Host above the chalice.

4. The angel gave the Host to Lucia.

5. The little shepherds saw a beautiful Lady.

6. Her heart had a circle of thorns.

7. A pearl rosary was in her hands.

8. The Lady asked the children to say the Rosary every day.

9. God gives graces through her Immaculate Heart.

Turn to Appendix for writing exercises.

Pray the Rosary every day.

More Subjects

A sentence is made of parts that together tell a complete idea.

A. Ask <u>who</u> or <u>what</u>. Then underline the subject.

1. <u>The Hebrews</u> were living in Egypt.

2. Cruel Pharaoh was keeping them as slaves.

3. The Hebrew slaves worked hard for Pharaoh.

4. Tall pyramids reached to the sky.

5. The hot sun beat down.

6. Desert winds blew sand on the slaves.

7. The people were suffering.

8. Moses cried out to God.

9. The rivers turned to blood.

10. Bugs flew into every house.

11. Frogs hopped everywhere.

12. Pharaoh had a hardened heart.

13. The Angel of Death passed over Egypt.

14. God's children are saved by the Lamb.

15. God hears the prayers of His people.

Predicates: One of Two Sentence Parts

A sentence is made of parts that together tell a complete idea. When two or more sentence parts are put together, they make a complete idea, or a complete sentence.

<u>who or what</u>   <u>doing</u>
The Hebrews   were living in Egypt.
The hot sun   beat down.

What were the Hebrews doing? They were living in Egypt. *Were living* is the action that the Hebrews are doing. *Were living in Egypt* is the *predicate* part of the sentence.

The hot sun *beat down*. *Beat down* is the <u>doing</u> part of the sentence. The <u>doing</u>, or action part, is called the *predicate* of the sentence.

A. Look for verbs. Then underline the predicate part of the sentence. [Hint: sometimes predicates just tell what is or was.]

1. A bush <u>burned in the desert.</u>

2. God spoke from the bush.

3. God's people had suffered.

4. Pharaoh was stubborn.

5. Soldiers chased the Hebrews.

6. The water opened up.

7. The Hebrews walked safely to the other side.

8. Moses took God's people to the Promised Land.

Photocopying of these pages is strictly illegal and a violation of copyright law.

Fun with Subjects and Predicates

A sentence is made of parts that together tell a complete idea.

When two or more sentence parts are put together, they make a complete idea, or a complete sentence.

The subject part of the sentence usually tells about a *who or what* noun.

The predicate part of the sentence has a verb that tells what happens.

A. Pick a subject part and pick a predicate part. Put them together to make a sentence. Print your sentence on the lines.

Subject	Predicate
The sleepy cat	is in the dollhouse.
My new bike	was pulled over my ears.
Jesse's warm hat	yawned and stretched.
Lucy's doll	filled my stomach.
That peanut butter sandwich	was speeding down the hill.

More Predicates

A sentence is made of parts that together tell a complete idea. When two or more sentence parts are put together, they make a complete idea, or a complete sentence.

A. Look for verbs. Then underline the predicate part of the sentence.

1. Agnes <u>grew up in Albania</u>.

2. Her family <u>loved Our Lord very much</u>.

3. Agnes' father <u>had died</u>.

4. Her mother <u>opened a store</u>.

5. She <u>sold cloth in the store</u>.

6. The children <u>worked hard</u>.

7. Agnes <u>helped teach little students</u>.

8. The Sisters of Our Lady of Loreto <u>invited her to visit</u>.

9. Agnes <u>wanted to serve God as a nun</u>.

10. She <u>travelled to India</u>.

11. This tiny nun <u>wanted to serve the poor</u>.

12. The Holy Father <u>gave his blessing</u>.

Do you know the religious name of this Sister?

Building Better Sentences

We can make more interesting sentences by putting parts from two or more sentences together.

Agnes sang at home.
Agnes sang at church.

Agnes sang at home and at church.

A. Build better sentences.

1. Agnes went on a picnic. Her brother Lazar went on the picnic, too.

2. Lazar ran down the hill. Lazar rolled in the grass.

3. Agnes picked wildflowers. Agnes gave the wildflowers to her mother.

Building Better Sentences

Build better sentences. Combine subjects.

1. St. Paul was in jail.
   Silas was in jail.

Build better sentences. Combine predicates.

2. St. Paul was praying joyfully.
   St. Paul was singing joyfully.

Build better sentences. Combine subjects.

3. The jailer asked to be baptized.
   His family asked to be baptized, also.

Beginning, Middle, and End

Stories have a beginning, a middle, and an end. You are learning to make interesting sentences. Now you can write an interesting story with beginning, middle, and end.

With your mom and dad, read the story of Elijah in 1 Kings 18:17-39 (3 Kings 18:17-39 in the Douay-Rheims). Tell the story in your own words. Then write your story.

What happens first?

_____
_____
_____
_____
_____
_____

What happens next?

_____
_____
_____
_____
_____
_____

What happens last?

_____
_____
_____
_____
_____
_____

Beginning, Middle, and End

You can write a story. Think about going to God's house to make your first confession. Your Father is always there to welcome you. Jesus waits longingly for your visit, and the Holy Spirit fills the church. Our Lady and all the angels and saints see that you have come to have your soul made beautiful...

Tell what happened [or might happen] first.

_____
_____
_____
_____

Tell what happened [or might happen] next.

_____
_____
_____
_____

Tell what happened [or might happen] last.

_____
_____
_____
_____

Photocopying of these pages is strictly illegal and a violation of copyright law.

Let's Review

A. Circle the verbs that show action.

1. cry   eat   am   was
2. make   is   sit   kick
3. are   break   were   leap

B. Circle the state of being verbs.

1. fix   eat   are   blow
2. am   destroy   strike   read
3. sunny   fly   is   poke

C. If the noun is possessive, add an apostrophe.

1. dogs collar
2. cats have fur
3. pair of glasses
4. two dogs
5. horses mane
6. Dads glasses
7. Fathers house
8. frogs in the pond
9. cats fur

D. Print 'C' for common nouns. Print 'P' for proper nouns.

1. ____ doctor
2. ____ city
3. ____ Baker City
4. ____ Eel Lake
5. ____ Doctor Green
6. ____ river

Turn to Appendix for writing exercises.

More Review

A. Circle 'S' for state of being verbs.   Circle 'A' for action verbs.

S A 1. It <u>is</u> the Feast of All Saints.

S A 2. Steve <u>was</u> Pope St. Gregory the Great.

S A 3. Luke <u>dressed</u> as St. Joseph.

S A 4. Mary and Julie <u>are</u> angels.

S A 5. Laura <u>wears</u> a crown.

B. Circle the helping verbs. Underline the verbs that show action. Then tell whether the sentence is past or present.

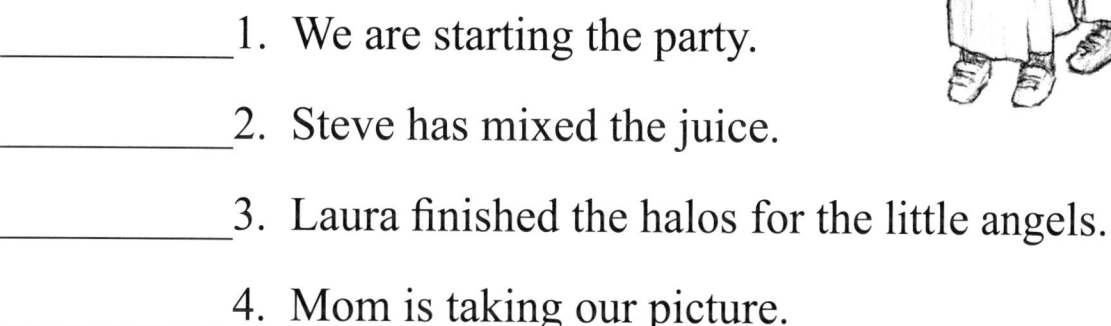

_____ 1. We are starting the party.

_____ 2. Steve has mixed the juice.

_____ 3. Laura finished the halos for the little angels.

_____ 4. Mom is taking our picture.

C. Circle the letters that need capitals. Print the capital letter above the circle.

1. beth and carmen live on bramble road.

2. i made my first holy communion at holy name church.

3. my uncle jack lives in lincoln, nebraska.

Turn to Appendix for writing exercises.

Roots and Verb Endings

The main part of a word is called a *root*. *Jump* and *roll* are root words. A *suffix* is a word part added at the end of a root. Common verb suffixes are *-ed* and *-ing*. Many words can add suffixes without changing the root.

A. Circle the root word.

1. (jump)ing
2. praying
3. pushed
4. bumped

B. Print the word. Add the suffix.

Root	-ing	-ed
pass		
bless		
reach		
smell		
greet		
talk		
walk		

Roots with Short Vowel/Consonant

Root words that end with a short vowel followed by a single consonant double the final consonant before adding the suffix.

run   running   pop   popping

A. Circle the root word.

1. popping
2. skipped
3. stopped
4. dripping

B. Print the word. Add the suffix.

Root	-ing	-ed
tap		
step		
pin		
slip		
snap		
beg		
bat		

Practice with Roots

A. Circle the root word. Remember the rules!

1. farming
2. wished
3. milked
4. matching
5. dressing
6. dragged
7. sledding
8. bragged

B. Print the word. Add the suffix.

Root	-ing	-ed
trap		
leap		
lick		
slip		
clap		
bag		
start		

Roots with Signal -e

Root words that end with signal -e drop the final -e before adding the suffix.

live   live[ed]   lived   liv[ing]   living

A. Print the root word.

1. living _____
2. hoping _____
3. adoring _____
4. praising _____

B. Print the word. Add the suffix.

Root	-ing	-ed
love		
bake		
promise		
care		
glue		
tape		
race		

Let's Review: Adding Suffixes

A. Circle the correct spelling.

Root

1. paste	pastted	pasted	passed
2. bike	biking	bikking	bikeing
3. wrap	wraping	wrapeing	wrapping
4. fast	fasted	fastted	fassted
5. wipe	wipeing	wiping	wipping
6. whip	whipped	whiped	whipd
7. live	living	liveing	livving
8. fast	fastting	fasting	fasteing
9. paste	pasting	pastting	pasteing
10. praise	praissed	praisedd	praised
11. set	seting	setting	seteing
12. sled	sleded	sledded	sledeted

B. Match the root word with its rule for adding a suffix.

slide   short vowel/single consonant end, double final consonant

hop   root that doesn't change with an added suffix

start   root that ends with signal -e, drop final -e before adding suffix

Prefixes

A *prefix* is a word part that is added to the front of the root word. *Prefixes change the meaning of the root word.*

prefix:	meaning:	
un-	not	*untrue* means not true
dis-	not	*disagree* means not agree
re-	again	*retry* means try again

A. Circle the root word.

1. untrue
2. reopen
3. untold
4. undo
5. distrust
6. retold

B. Add a prefix to the underlined word to make a new word.

This word means 'close again.' reclose

This word means 'not obey.'

This word means 'make again.'

This word means 'not opened.'

This word means 'not heard.'

More Prefixes

Prefixes can add interest to our writing. Instead of saying, "I trust in God, Whom I can not see," we may say, "I trust in God, Who is unseen." Prefixes give us another way to tell what we want to say.

> "...we look not to the things that are seen but to the things that are unseen..."
> 2 Cor. 4:18

prefix:	meaning:
un-	not
dis-	not
re-	again

A. Circle the root word.

1. unseen
2. unable
3. dislike
4. redo
5. dishonest
6. repay

B. Add a prefix to the underlined word to make a new word.

This word means 'fold again.'

This word means 'not happy.'

This word means 'try again.'

This word means 'not kind.'

This word means 'not seen.'

Contractions

Like prefixes, *contractions* can also add variety to our writing. Instead of saying, "St. Gemma is sick," we might say, "St. Gemma *isn't* well."

	Contraction
is not	isn't
are not	aren't
was not	wasn't
were not	weren't
did not	didn't
could not	couldn't
would not	wouldn't
should not	shouldn't
has not	hasn't
have not	haven't
let us	let's

A. Print the two words that mean the same as the contraction.

wouldn't _____

didn't _____

isn't _____

let's _____

wasn't _____

"...let us not grow weary of doing good..."

Galatians 6:9

Using Contractions

A. Read the first sentence in each pair. Print the contraction that will make the second sentence say the same thing as the first, but in a different way.

1. Bridget remembers to thank God for His blessings.

   Bridget [did not] **didn't** forget to thank God for His blessings.

2. Our Lord always remembers His children.

   Our Lord [has not] _____ forgotten His children.

3. Shall we check Bridget's table manners?

   [Let us]_____ check Bridget's table manners.

4. Bridget eats her soup slowly and neatly.

   Bridget [should not]_____ gobble or slurp her soup.

5. Bridget wipes her hands on the napkin.

   Bridget [is not] _____ wiping her hands on the tablecloth.

6. This child ate without spilling a drop.

   This child [was not] _____ sloppy.

7. Her clothes are still fresh and clean.

   Her clothes [are not] _____ dirty.

   Good job, Bridget! You remembered your manners!

Turn to Appendix for writing exercises.

Syllables

Words can often be broken into parts called *syllables*. *A syllable is a group of letters having only one vowel sound.*

Pup has one vowel sound. It is a one-syllable word.

Train has two vowels, but they form a blend that makes only one sound. *Train* is also a one-syllable word.

Letter has two vowel sounds. It is a two-syllable word. We might divide the word into syllables like this: *let ter*

Favor has two vowel sounds. It is a two-syllable word. Each syllable has one vowel sound: *fa vor*

Learning about syllables can help you to become a better speller. Knowing about syllables can also help you to better understand poetry.

A. How many vowel sounds do you hear? Say the word. Clap your hands with each syllable that you hear. Then tell how many syllables you hear in these words.

__2__ driving	_____ sing	_____ Maker
_____ eat	_____ later	_____ holy
_____ napkin	_____ sheep	_____ saint

B. Underline the vowel <u>sounds</u> that you hear. [Remember that two vowels together often blend to make <u>one</u> sound.]

    r<u>ea</u>d   student   his

    garden   pop   speed

Turn to Appendix for writing exercises.

Words that Rhyme

Rhyming words are often found in poetry.
Rhyming words have the same ending sounds.

Heart of Jesus, I <u>adore Thee</u>
    Heart of Mary, I <u>implore Thee</u>
Heart of Joseph, pure and <u>just</u>
    In these three Hearts, I place my <u>trust</u>.

A. Circle the word that rhymes with the word on the left.

1. just	rest	(trust)	heart	last
2. rest	bake	dwell	trust	west
3. last	pin	fast	sat	rest
4. cry	land	dry	sat	pin
5. night	make	man	fight	me
6. tree	dry	land	sat	free
7. sin	free	man	pin	cake
8. flood	land	blood	water	bell
9. hill	still	hat	held	bail
10. mail	free	bail	might	letter
11. better	best	man	rest	letter
12. raise	try	praise	rise	tries

Syllables and Rhyme

THE CHILDREN AND THE ANGELS
by Mary E. Mannix

When little children laugh and <u>play</u>, _____

'Mid snares and perils of the <u>day</u>, _____

The guardian angels stand <u>between</u> _____

Each lure and pitfall dark, <u>unseen</u>. _____

A. **Write the number of syllables in the underlined words above.** Can you see that matching rhymes and syllables make this poem pleasing?

B. **Draw lines to connect the words that rhyme.**

side	far	bed	raise
star	mild	praise	me
child	guide	be	head

C. **Using some of the words from the columns above, can you finish this poem? Print the rhyming words on the lines.**

DEAR ANGEL, EVER AT MY SIDE
Father Frederick William Faber *[1814-1863]*

Dear angel, ever at my side,

How loving thou must be,

To leave thy home in Heaven to_____ [rhymes with 'side']

A little child like_____. [rhymes with 'be']

DON'T GIVE UP

Phoebe Cary [1824-1871]

If you've tried and have not won,
    Never stop for crying;
All that's great and good is done
    Just by patient trying.

Though young birds, in flying, fall,
    Still their wings grow stronger;
And the next time they can keep
    Up a little longer.

If by easy work you beat,
    Who the more will prize you?
Gaining victory from defeat,
    That's the test that tries you!

Syllable Practice

A syllable is a group of letters having only one vowel sound.

A. **How many vowel sounds do you hear? Say the word. Clap your hands with each syllable that you hear. Then tell how many syllables you hear in these words. Remember that** *signal e*, **which appears at the end of the word, is silent.**

_____ bread   _____ ram   _____ net

_____ bake   _____ lost   _____ boat

_____ baker   _____ shepherd   _____ fishing

_____ pan   _____ find   _____ river

_____ cupcake   _____ comfort   _____ hook

B. **Underline the vowel sounds that you hear. Remember that two vowels together often blend to make <u>one</u> sound. Do you remember that 'y' often acts as a vowel?**

baby	Lady	pope
sleepy	faith	leader
angel	Virgin	church
watch	pure	speak
bedside	Mother	listen
guard	holy	obey

Adjectives: Telling about Nouns

Nouns name people, places, and things.
baby
Words that tell about nouns are called *adjectives*.

tiny baby   **new** baby   **sleepy** baby

What kind of baby? A *tiny, new, sleepy* baby. *Tiny, new,* and *sleepy* are **adjectives** that tell about the noun.

A. Underline the nouns. Then circle the adjectives.

1. The (tiny) baby has a (lacy) bonnet.
2. The baby wears a white dress for her baptism.
3. Cool water was poured on her little forehead.
4. Feel the soft skin of the quiet infant.
5. Mary Katherine is a sweet baby with a beautiful soul.

B. Cross out the words that are NOT adjectives.

~~water~~	hot	~~faucet~~
cupcake	tasty	sticky
scratchy	blue	sweater
rosary	holy	pray
funny	book	pages
mouse	squeaky	cheese

More Adjectives

A. Nouns name people, places, and things.
Underline nouns in the sentences.

B. Adjectives tell about nouns.
Circle the adjectives in the sentences.

1. <u>Nick</u> belongs to a (busy) <u>family</u>.
2. His happy family works together on a huge farm.
3. His little brother feeds the plump pigs.
4. Nick carries heavy buckets of cracked corn to the pen.
5. His older sister waters the red hens.
6. Then she collects the fresh eggs in an old, tin pan.
7. Mother cracks the brown eggs into a shiny skillet.
8. Soon, the family sits down to a hot breakfast.
9. Next, Nick will feed the young calves.
10. He mixes warm milk in a metal pail.
11. Nick kneels on the hard floor of the old barn.
12. The greedy calves push to get a turn.
13. Sticky milk spills onto his blue jeans.
14. Clean, dry hay is pitched into a wooden manger.
15. When we sit down to a tasty meal, we thank our good God.
16. We can also thank God for strong families on the farm.

Fun with Adjectives

A. Adjectives add interest to what we write and say. You can make this story more interesting. Print the story on the lines below. Where you find a star in the story, print one or two adjectives in its place. You may pick adjectives from the word box, or you may choose your own adjectives. Is the second story more interesting than the first story?

Will was a ✸ boy. One ✸ day, he went down to the ✸ river for a ✸ swim. He merrily leaped into the ✸ water. Will took a ✸ breath. He swam under the ✸ water. Then Will opened his eyes wide and saw a [an] ✸ fish staring back at him. Will's ✸ arms flashed as he swam back to the ✸ riverbank.

weak	strong	hot	warm	freezing	deep	huge	dinky	long
short	ugly	clear	slimy	mighty	safe	sunny	dark	silly
scary	strange	brave	bright	muddy	green	sandy	cheerful	

Example: Will was a <u>strong, cheerful</u> boy.

Adjectives that Compare

Adjectives are words that tell about nouns.
When two nouns are compared, the suffix *-er* is added to the root word.

long dog   *longer dog*

When three or more nouns are compared, the suffix *-est* is added.

long   *longer*   *longest*

It is not difficult to remember when to use *-er* or *-est*. When comparing two things, use the suffix with two letters: *-er*. When comparing three or more, use the suffix with three letters: *-est*.

A. Print the root word, adding the correct suffix.

1. Jess runs [fast] _____ than Eric.

2. Annie is the [fast] _____ runner in the group.

3. The moon is [bright] _____ tonight than it was last night.

4. Aaron is the [tall] _____ altar boy in our whole parish.

5. Emily is the [kind] _____ girl on our street.

Adjectives that Compare

The first child in the parade is tallest.

A. Print the root word. Add the correct suffix.

1. The child with the drum is [short] _____ than the first boy.

2. The girl with the flag is the [short] _____ of all.

3. Is the horn [loud] _____ than the drum?

4. The boy with the horn is [close] _____ to the big flags.

5. The flag held by the little girl is [small] _____ of all.

6. The Vatican flag is the [high] _____ of three flags.

7. Have you seen a parade [long] _____ than this one?

8. Is it [safe] _____ to march in the yard, in the street, or on the sidewalk?

9. Which special day is [close] _____ to autumn: the Fourth of July, or the Feast of the Assumption?

10. Of the two, which is the [fine] _____ day to celebrate?

Turn to Appendix for writing exercises.

Let's Review

A. Tell whether the verb is past or present.

_____ 1. Adam and Eve <u>lost</u> everything.

_____ 2. Jesus <u>came</u> to save us.

_____ 3. God <u>gives</u> freely.

_____ 4. Our Lord <u>created</u> us to share in His divine life.

_____ 5. We <u>praise</u> God for His mercy and love.

B. If the sentence is marked 'S,' underline the subject. If it is marked 'P,' underline the predicate.

__S__ 1. Our Lord gave to His followers the power to forgive sins.

__P__ 2. John tells his sins to the priest.

__P__ 3. This boy has made a good confession.

C. Circle the helping verbs. Underline the verbs that show action.

1. He had asked the Holy Spirit for help.

2. Now he has said his penance.

3. John went home with a light heart and a clean soul.

Turn to Appendix for writing exercises.

More Review

A. Circle the root word.

1. burning
2. pumped
3. climbing
4. called

B. Add the suffix -ing.

5. spray_____
6. drag_____
7. drip_____
8. slip_____

C. Add the prefix that means 'do again' to each word. Print the new word.

play _____   make _____

print _____   open _____

D. Add a prefix that means 'not' to each word. Print the new word.

like _____   do _____

E. Tell the number of syllables.

1. _____ flames
2. _____ hose
3. _____ ladder
4. _____ raincoat
5. _____ truck
6. _____ water

Pronouns Take the Place of Nouns

Nouns name people, places, and things. *Pronouns* take the place of nouns.

nouns: *Stephen and Paul* will serve at Holy Mass.
pronoun: *They* will serve at Holy Mass.

They, *them,* and *their* tell about more than one.

Other pronouns are: *he she it him her his*

Her, his, and *their* are pronouns that show possession.

Father's vestments=*his* vestments   Stephen and Paul's house= *their* house

A. Cross out the nouns in the box. Print the correct pronoun.

1. [Father Wilbert] __He__ is a Franciscan priest.

2. Father Wilbert has faithfully served [Jesus] _____ for sixty years.

3. A crowd of [Father's] _____ friends have come for Holy Mass.

4. [The church] _____ is filled with people.

5. Many of [the people] _____ had been baptized long ago by Father.

6. [Father Wilbert] _____ had married a number of the couples.

7. Father had also baptized many of [the people's] _____ children.

8. Now [the people] _____ have come to honor [the priest] _____.

Photocopying of these pages is strictly illegal and a violation of copyright law.

Capital Letters and Pronouns that Take the Place of God's Name

Sometimes when we speak of God, we use pronouns to take the place of His Name. We may say, "Blessed be God's holy Name." We can also say, "Blessed be His holy Name." The pronoun His takes the place of the word God. A traditional way to show honor and respect for God is to capitalize words that take the place of His holy Name.

A. The words in the box below can be used in place of God's Name. Some of the sentences below use the words in the box to take the place of God's Name. Other sentences use *him*, *his*, and *he* to take the place of a boy's name. When pronouns are used in place of a *person's* name, they are *not* capitalized. **If the pronouns in the sentence need capitals, print 'yes' in front of the sentence. If the pronouns do not need capitals, print 'no.' Then circle the words that need capitals. Print the capital above the circle. The first two sentences have been done for you.**

Him His He Thee Thy

1. __yes__ My strength is the Lord; (he) is my Savior. [H above "he"]

2. __no__ Mark put his shirts in the drawer.

3. _____ Give thanks to the Lord; tell of his wonderful deeds.

4. _____ Sing a new song to the Lord; give him the praise that is due.

5. _____ Mark says that these socks belong to him.

6. _____ We praise thee, O God, in thy holy place.

7. _____ thy kingdom come, thy will be done on earth as it is in Heaven.

Pronouns: Me and I

Pronouns take the place of nouns. Pronouns often take the place of names. The pronouns *I* and *me* have their own special places in sentences. *I* is part of the subject and comes before a verb. *Me* is part of the predicate and comes after a verb.

Subject	Predicate
I	walked to Grandma's house.
Subject	Predicate
That dog	followed *me*.

When *I* share the subject with another person, I always put myself last.

Jenny and I   went to the parish bazaar.

A. Print the correct pronoun.

1. Jenny and [me I] _____ bought red balloons.

2. Dominic held the balloon for [me I] _____.

3. Jenny and [me I] _____ like cherry snow cones.

4. Mother gave [me I] _____ two dollars to spend.

5. Father told [me I] _____ that the bazaar was for the food bank.

6. Dominic and [me I] _____ sometimes help in the kitchen.

7. He and [me I] _____ wash dishes and clear the tables.

Pronouns: They, We, Us and Them

The pronouns *they, we, us,* and *them* take the place of more than one noun. These pronouns have their own special places in sentences. *We* and *they* are part of the subject and come before a verb. *Us* and *them* are part of the predicate and come after a verb.

	Subject	*Predicate*	
[John and I]	We	sang at the nursing home.	
	The residents	were glad to see *us*.	[John and I]
[the residents]	They	sang along.	
	John and I	like singing for *them*.	[the residents]

| we | us | they | them |

A.   Print the correct pronoun in place of the boxed word or words.

1. [Lupe and I] _____ read about the life of St. Francis of Assisi.

2. Aunt Frances gave the book to [Lupe and me] _____.

3. St. Francis wanted to win [the Muslims] _____ to the Faith.

4. [The Muslims] _____ did not harm him.

5. [St. Francis and his followers] _____ fed the poor.

6. He nursed the sick and gave medicine to [the sick] _____.

7. Mother helped [Lupe and me] _____ write a thank-you note.

8. Now [Lupe and I] _____ are writing a book report.

Pronouns and You

You is a pronoun that can take the place of one or more than one noun.

You are my grandparents.   *You* are a bus driver.

A. Underline <u>you</u> in the sentence. Print 'one' if it means one person, or 'more' if more than one person.

1. _____ You are my brothers and sisters.

2. _____ You are my child.

3. _____ You have a servant's heart.

B. Print the correct pronoun on the line.

> them   they   we   us   Him   her   His   He   She

1. [St. Margaret Mary] _____ had a vision of Jesus.

2. [Jesus] _____ asked [St. Margaret Mary] _____ to tell people to trust in [Jesus'] _____ Sacred Heart.

3. At first, [the people] _____ did not believe St. Margaret Mary.

4. Now, First Friday is set aside to honor [the Sacred Heart] _____.

5. Jesus made twelve promises to [you and me] _____.

6. [You and I] _____ will be blessed if we do what Jesus asks.

7. [People] _____ should receive Holy Communion on First Fridays.

8. Our Lord will give graces to [the people] _____.

Photocopying of these pages is strictly illegal and a violation of copyright law.

Mixed Pronoun Practice

A. Print the pronoun that can be used in place of the underlined noun.

1. _____ You and I are in second grade.

2. _____ Sister Anthony is teaching you and me about confession.

3. _____ Our parents bring us to class each Wednesday afternoon.

B. Print the correct pronoun on the line.

| Him them they it we us him her his he she |

1. [This morning] _____ is a beautiful morning.

2. Our Lord has given [you and me] _____ a new day.

3. [Mike and Molly] _____ have just said their Morning Offering.

4. Now Mike tosses [Mike's] _____ pillow at [Molly] _____ .

5. [Molly] _____ is not mad at [Mike] _____ .

6. [Molly and Mike] _____ have fun but they are kind to each other.

7. Jesus loves [these children] _____ and they love [Jesus] _____ .

Abbreviation of Days and Months

Both months and days of the week have names which are capitalized. Because we use these names often, it is helpful to use *abbreviations*, or shorter forms, of these words. *Abbreviations* end with a period.

Days of the Week
Sunday = Sun.
Monday = Mon.
Tuesday = Tues.
Wednesday = Wed.
Thursday = Thurs.
Friday = Fri.
Saturday = Sat.
Months of the Year
January = Jan.
February = Feb.
March = Mar.
April = Apr.
May = [May]
June = [June]
July = [July]
August = Aug.
September = Sept.
October = Oct.
November = Nov.
December = Dec.

A. Match the abbreviations with the names of the months and days of the week. Notice that May, June, and July are not abbreviated.

January	Oct.
February	Aug.
March	Dec.
April	Jan.
May	Sept.
June	Mar.
July	Feb.
August	June
September	Nov.
October	May
November	Apr.
December	July
Sunday	Fri.
Monday	Sat.
Tuesday	Thurs.
Wednesday	Mon.
Thursday	Sun.
Friday	Tues.
Saturday	Wed.

Abbreviations

How good Our Lord is to have given us life and days to praise His mercy! Let us use each day to glorify Him.

A. Print the abbreviation on the line.

1. [January]_____ honors the Holy Name.

2. [May] _____ belongs to Our Lady.

3. [Sunday]_____ honors the Holy Trinity.

4. Of course, Ash Wednesday always falls on a [Wednesday]_____!

5. The month of [June] _____ gives glory to the Sacred Heart.

6. The Church fixes [March] _____ as the Month of St. Joseph.

7. On [Monday]_____ we honor the Holy Angels.

8. The Feast of the Our Lady of the Rosary falls in [October]_____.

9. The Month of the Holy Souls is [November]_____.

10. Each [Tuesday] _____ is dedicated to the Apostles.

11. Can you guess the Person honored in [December]_____?

12. Our Lady's Immaculate Heart is honored in [August]_____.

13. [February]_____ is the Month of the Passion of Our Lord.

14. In the month of [April]_____ we honor the Holy Eucharist.

Turn to Appendix for writing exercises.

More Abbreviations

Blessed = Bl.   Saint = St.   Road = Rd.   Street = St.

North = N.   South = S.   East = E.   West = W.

Can you guess why these abbreviations are capitalized? It is because they are used with proper nouns. They are only used with the names of specific people and streets.

Bl. Imelda   *St.* Dominic Savio

Many abbreviations used in arithmetic and science are not capitalized, such as:

inch = in. [6 in.]   foot = ft. [3 ft.]

When these abbreviations are plural, no 's' is added at the end.

A. Print the abbreviation on the line.

1. The parents of [Saint] _____ Therese have been declared saints.

2. They are [Saint] _____ Zelie and [Saint] _____ Louis Martin.

3. Pine [Street] _____ is two blocks away.

4. We live at 132 Barton [Road] _____ , in a yellow house.

5. Our church is on [North] _____ Elm [Street] _____ .

6. My grandfather lives in [East] _____ [Saint] _____ Louis.

7. [Blessed] _____ Miguel Pro was beatified in 1988.

Turn to Appendix for writing exercises.

Titles of Respect

When we speak or write to adults, we show respect by using titles with their names.

We say:	Abbreviation:	We show respect to:
Mister	Mr.	a man
Missus	Mrs.	a married woman
Miss	Miss	an unmarried woman
Doctor	Dr.	a doctor
Father	Fr.	a priest
Sister	Sr.	a religious sister

A. Match the title that we say with its abbreviation.

We say:	We write:
Sister	Mr.
Father	Mrs.
Doctor	Miss
Missus	Dr.
Miss	Fr.
Mister	Sr.

B. Print the correct title in the blank. Remember to capitalize.

1. [Missus] **Mrs.** Cook babysits at our house.

2. [Sister] _____ Lucia points us to Our Lady of Fatima.

3. [Doctor] _____ Vincent took off my cast.

4. [Mister] _____ Evans changed the oil in our car.

5. [Father] Our parish priest is _____ Pius Brazauskas.

Initials

When we address an envelope, we seldom use a person's full name. Instead, we often use *initials*. An *initial* is the first letter of a word. Initials are usually followed by a period.

Robert Joseph Johnson's initials are: R.J.J.

A letter addressed to him might read: Mr. R.J. Johnson

A.

Print your initials on the first line.

Print your first two initials and your last name on the second line.

Print your mother's initials here.

Print your father's initials here.

There are other special initials that make us think of Our Lord and Lady and the saints. It is good to print these initials on our school papers. They can remind us that all our work and play is done with and for God.

B. Match the initials.

Jesus, Mary, Joseph	M.G.I.L.T.
Ad Majorem Dei Gloriam [This means 'All to the Greater Glory of God']	A.F.T.D.J.
My God, I Love Thee	J.M.J.
All for Thee, Dear Jesus	A.M.D.G.

Abbreviation of States

The names of states are capitalized. Their special abbreviations *do not* end with periods.

Alabama	AL	Montana	MT
Alaska	AK	Nebraska	NE
Arizona	AZ	Nevada	NV
Arkansas	AR	New Hampshire	NH
California	CA	New Jersey	NJ
Colorado	CO	New Mexico	NM
Connecticut	CT	New York	NY
Delaware	DE	North Carolina	NC
Florida	FL	North Dakota	ND
Georgia	GA	Ohio	OH
Hawaii	HI	Oklahoma	OK
Idaho	ID	Oregon	OR
Illinois	IL	Pennsylvania	PA
Indiana	IN	Rhode Island	RI
Iowa	IA	South Carolina	SC
Kansas	KS	South Dakota	SD
Kentucky	KY	Tennessee	TN
Louisiana	LA	Texas	TX
Maine	ME	Utah	UT
Maryland	MD	Vermont	VT
Massachusetts	MA	Virginia	VA
Michigan	MI	Washington	WA
Minnesota	MN	West Virginia	WV
Mississippi	MS	Wisconsin	WI
Missouri	MO	Wyoming	WY

```
Your Name
Street Address
City, State   Zip
         Your Friend's Name
         Street Address
         City, State   Zip Code
```

Practicing Addresses

<u>Mister</u> Daniel Aranda
1302 Mountain <u>Street</u>
Lebanon, <u>Oregon</u>   55379

A. Print this address on the lines below. Use the correct abbreviation for each underlined word.

_____
_____
_____
_____

Address Practice

A. Use the correct abbreviation for each underlined word. Print your name and address in the proper place.

Address this envelope to:
<u>Missus</u> Mary Tillotson
2320 Brownbush <u>Road</u>
Skey, <u>Missouri</u>   07794

B. Print your grandparents' address on the envelope below. Remember your address, too.

Letter Writing

These are the parts that make up a letter. You can write a letter to your parish priest or to a religious, thanking them for their service to the Body of Christ. Practice first on this page. Read your letter carefully. Are there any sentences that can be combined? Can you add adjectives or synonyms for interest? Make a 'best' copy of your letter to send.

Dedication: J.M.J.

*Date:*_____

Greeting: Dear_____,

Body:

Closing: [Sincerely,] [God bless,]

*Your Signature:*_____

Learning About Books

A *title* is the name of a book. Most words in a title are capitalized. [Small words like *a, an, the, in,* and *of* are not capitalized in titles.] When we write about a book, we always underline the title.

An *author* is the person who writes the book.

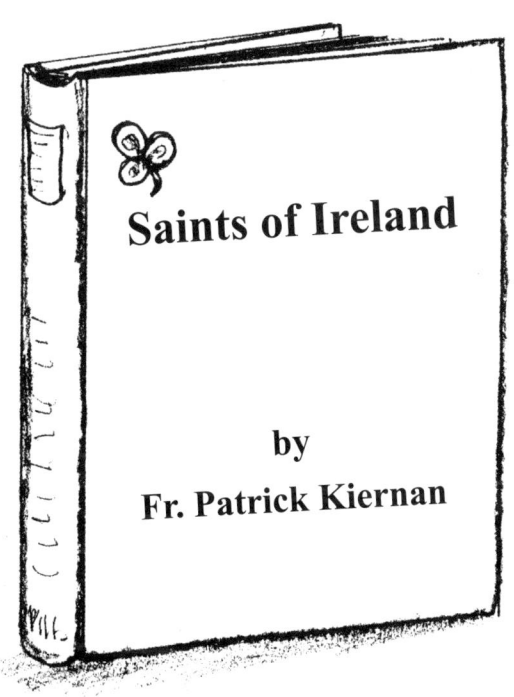

A. **Print and underline the book's title.**

_____

Print the name of the author.

_____

B. **Print the titles and authors of your three favorite books. Remember to underline and capitalize.**

_____
_____
_____
_____
_____

Table of Contents

A book's *table of contents* tells what is in the book. It also tells on which page information can be found.

Table of Contents	Page
Pirates!..2	
St. Patrick in Chains..............................5	
A Voice From Heaven 9	
A Priest Forever..................................12	
St. Patrick and the Trinity....................14	
St. Kilian Writes About St. Brigid..........15	
The Picts Are Converted.....................17	
St. Kenan Builds a Cathedral...............22	

A.

1. On which page will you find information about St. Patrick's capture by pirates?

2. Which page might have information about St. Columba teaching the Picts?

3. Which page might have information about how St. Patrick became a priest?

4. Which page might tell about the first stone cathedral in Ireland?

5. On which page might you find information about the life of St. Brigid?

Order and the Alphabet

The dictionary, the encyclopedia, telephone books, and the parish directory all use ABC order. Learning how to put words in ABC order will help us to find words and topics easily.

These mixed-up letters have been put in order. ABC order does not always use all letters. Can you see that the letters N and O are missing?

Q M P = M̲ __ __ P̲ Q̲

A B C D E F G H I J K L M N O P Q R S T U V W X Y Z

Letters can be put in ABC order. Words can be put in ABC order, too. Look at the first letter of the word. **Put the words in ABC order. Print the words in ABC order on the lines below. Some letters of the alphabet are not used.**

Patrick   _____

Trinity   _____

miracles   _____

convert   _____

shamrock   _____

Ireland   _____

baptized   _____

St. Patrick, pray for us

Photocopying of these pages is strictly illegal and a violation of copyright law.

Alphabetizing to the Second Letter

A B C D E F G H I J K L M N O P Q R S T U V W X Y Z

You can put words that begin with different letters in alphabetical order. To alphabetize words that begin with the same letter, look at the *second* letter. Then alphabetize to the *second* letter.

Not in alphabetical order: b**i**shop   b**a**ptism   b**o**ys

In alphabetical order: b**a**ptism   b**i**shop   b**o**ys

Put the words in ABC order to the second letter.

A.

Lourdes   _____

life   _____

lady   _____

least   _____

B.

field   _____

Fatima   _____

friends   _____

flames   _____

C.   ask   _____

angel   _____

after   _____

Alphabetizing to the Second Letter

Alphabetize to the *second* letter.

A.

drink _____

damp _____

dog _____

B.

wrist _____

wet _____

wipe _____

wagon _____

C.

bless _____

born _____

birth _____

baby _____

D.

medal _____

Mother _____

miracle _____

Mary _____

E.

cookies _____

cracker _____

candy _____

cupcake _____

Photocopying of these pages is strictly illegal and a violation of copyright law.

Alphabetizing and the Dictionary

To use a dictionary, you will need to alphabetize and put words in order by the second letter.

Can you see which word belongs in between the two boxed words?

-pear
-prize

place

paper

First, look at the second letters of *pear* and *prize*. They are *e* and *r*. The second letters of *place* and *paper* are *l* and *a*. Because *l* comes between *e* and *r* in the alphabet, *place* is the word that belongs between the two words.

Which word belongs between? Print the words from the circle in the correct boxes.

1. -mice
   -
   -mud

2. -seat
   -
   -slide

3. -slide
   -
   -stand

(tent, smile, sit, trip, meal, mouth)

4. -march
   -
   -mice

5. -tail
   -
   -torn

6. -toss
   -
   -tub

Dictionary Guide Words

Alphabetizing to the second letter is useful when you use dictionary *guide words*. *Guide words* show the reader which words can be found on that page. [Can you find the guide words in a dictionary?]

The guide word at the top left hand corner tells which word comes first on the page. The guide word at the top right hand corner tells which word comes last on the page. *Beat* is the first word found on this page. *Break* is the last word found on this page. The second letter in *beat* is *e*. The second letter in *break* is *r*. All the rest of the words on this page must have second letters between *e* and *r*.

beat	break
(beat)	bite
—	—
—	—
bend	brand
—	—
—	—
bird	—
—	(break)
—	—

Which words belong between the guide words on these pages? Print the words from the circle on the correct pages. Put the words in alphabetical order.

page #1

sack	smart
1. _____	
2. _____	
3. _____	
4. _____	

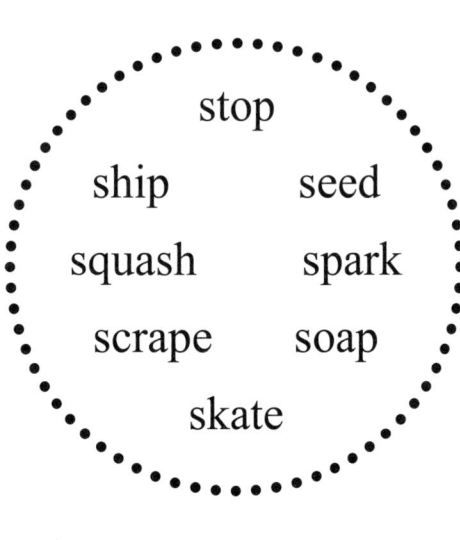

page #2

snake	swim
1. _____	
2. _____	
3. _____	
4. _____	

Let's Review

A. Print the correct pronoun to take the place of the underlined words.

1. For the sake of <u>Jesus'</u> [His   Him] _____ sorrowful Passion....

2. ...have mercy on <u>Maria, John and on me</u> [we   us] _____....

3. <u>Luke and I</u> [we   us] _____ found a purse in the street.

4. The purse didn't belong to <u>Luke and I</u> [we   us] _____.

5. <u>These coins</u> [they   them] _____ must belong to Mrs. Low.

6. We can return <u>the coins</u> [they   them] _____ to her now!

B. Print the correct pronoun.

1. Laura and [me   I] _____ baked blueberry bread.

2. The pan was too hot for [me   I] _____.

3. [She   Her] _____ lifted the pan with pot holders.

4. [me   I] _____ can help slice the bread.

C. Circle the pronouns that need capitals. Print the capital above the circle.

1. Mark shared his race cars with me.

2. Glory to God; may we sing his praises forever.

3. thy word is a lamp to my feet.

More Review

A. Print an abbreviation or title in place of the underlined words.

1. In <u>August,</u> _____ we are taking a trip.

2. <u>Father</u> _____ Greg is driving our family to <u>Michigan</u> _____.

3. There, <u>Mister</u> _____ Stone will take us to see Our Lady's grotto.

4. Assumption Grotto is on Gratiot <u>Street</u> _____.

5. We will also visit <u>Saint</u> _____ Jude Church.

6. It is at 3455 Assumption <u>Road</u> _____, <u>North</u> _____ <u>East</u> _____.

B. Print and underline the book titles correctly on the lines below. Remember capitals.

the children of fatima

_____

the king of the golden city

_____

little house on the prairie

_____

the little princess

_____

TAKE MY BODY, JESUS

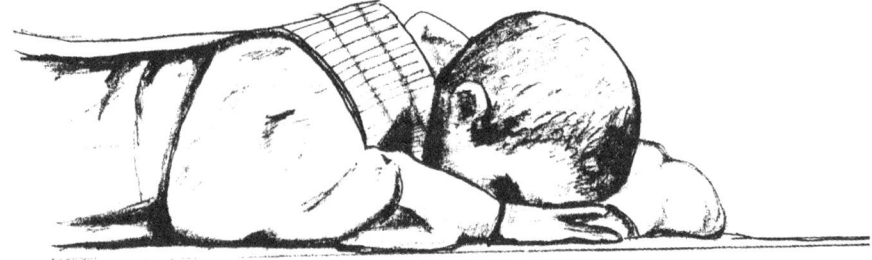

Take my body, Jesus,
    Eyes and ears and tongue;

Never let them, Jesus,
    Help to do Thee wrong.

Take my heart and fill it
    Full of love for Thee.

All I have, I give Thee:
    Give Thyself to me.

—Anonymous

Do you resolve... to consecrate yourselves to God for the salvation of all?

You are a priest forever, according to the order of Melchisedech.

from the Ritual Mass for Ordination and Ps. 110:4

Appendix: Review Exercises

My Journal Page

[Assign after page 20 has been completed.]

Write two or three sentences telling about an extra hot day in summer. What did you do to cool down? Use the word 'hot' in the first sentence. Use a synonym for 'hot' in your second or third sentence. Be sure to use capitals and proper punctuation.

Copywork and Dictation

[Assign after page 21 has been completed.]

Select three sentences from a favorite book. Discuss punctuation, capitalization, and spelling of any unfamiliar words with your teacher. Then copy the sentences on the lines below.

When you have finished, your teacher will dictate to you the same sentences for writing and grammar practice. [Please write dictated sentences on a separate sheet.] After your teacher has dictated these sentences to you, check your work by comparing it with the sentences in the book. Be sure to note capitalizations and punctuation. [If the teacher prefers, the student may read the sentences, slowly, into a digital recorder, then substitute the recording for teacher dictation.]

Be sure to turn to page 1 for more practice exercises.

My Journal Page

[Assign after page 30 has been completed.]

Write about what you might do if Jesus came to your house. When you are done writing, circle the nouns and underline the proper nouns in your sentences.

Copywork and Dictation

[Assign after page 31 has been completed.]

Select three sentences from a favorite book. Discuss punctuation, capitalization, and spelling of any unfamiliar words with your teacher. Identify nouns. Then copy the sentences on the lines below.

When you have finished, your teacher will dictate to you the same sentences for writing and grammar practice. [Please write dictated sentences on a separate sheet.] After your teacher has dictated these sentences to you, check your work by comparing it with the sentences in the book. Be sure to note capitalizations and punctuation. [If the teacher prefers, the student may read the sentences, slowly, into a digital recorder, then substitute the recording for teacher dictation.]

Be sure to turn to page 1 for more practice exercises.

My Journal Page

[Assign after page 40 has been completed.]

Write about your favorite animals. How do the animals move or play? Are they frisky or speedy? When you are done writing, circle the nouns and underline the verbs in your sentences.

Copywork and Dictation

[Assign after page 41 has been completed.]

Select three sentences from a favorite book. Discuss punctuation, capitalization, and spelling of any unfamiliar words with your teacher. Identify nouns. Then copy the sentences on the lines below.

When you have finished, your teacher will dictate to you the same sentences for writing and grammar practice. [Please write dictated sentences on a separate sheet.] After your teacher has dictated these sentences to you, check your work by comparing it with the sentences in the book. Be sure to note capitalizations and punctuation. [If the teacher prefers, the student may read the sentences, slowly, into a digital recorder, then substitute the recording for teacher dictation.]

Be sure to turn to page 1 for more practice exercises.

My Journal Page

[Assign after page 50 has been completed.]

What would you like to see if you visited Peru? Write a few sentences about your trip and places or things you might see. When you are done writing, circle nouns and underline proper nouns. Draw a box around verbs.

Copywork and Dictation

[Assign after page 51 has been completed.]

Select three sentences from a favorite book. Discuss punctuation, capitalization, and spelling of any unfamiliar words with your teacher. Identify nouns. Then copy the sentences on the lines below.

When you have finished, your teacher will dictate to you the same sentences for writing and grammar practice. [Please write dictated sentences on a separate sheet.] After your teacher has dictated these sentences to you, check your work by comparing it with the sentences in the book. Be sure to note capitalizations and punctuation. [If the teacher prefers, the student may read the sentences, slowly, into a digital recorder, then substitute the recording for teacher dictation.]

Be sure to turn to page 1 for more practice exercises.

My Journal Page

[Assign after page 60 has been completed.]

If your family travelled to Italy, what would they pack for the trip? Pick one family member. Tell what he or she might bring and why. Use his or her name, and remember to use proper punctuation and capitalization. If you use a possessive, be sure to include the apostrophe!

Copywork and Dictation

[Assign after page 61 has been completed.]

Select three sentences from a favorite book. Discuss punctuation, capitalization, and spelling of any unfamiliar words with your teacher. Identify nouns. Then copy the sentences on the lines below.

When you have finished, your teacher will dictate to you the same sentences for writing and grammar practice. [Please write dictated sentences on a separate sheet.] After your teacher has dictated these sentences to you, check your work by comparing it with the sentences in the book. Be sure to note capitalizations and punctuation. [If the teacher prefers, the student may read the sentences, slowly, into a digital recorder, then substitute the recording for teacher dictation.]

Be sure to turn to page 1 for more practice exercises.

My Journal Page

[Assign after page 70 has been completed.]

Tell about playing outside last summer. Did you ride a bike, or swim, or go hiking? Be sure to use past tense verbs. Underline all the verbs when you are done writing.

_____
_____
_____
_____
_____
_____
_____
_____
_____
_____
_____
_____
_____
_____
_____
_____
_____
_____

Copywork and Dictation

[Assign after page 71 has been completed.]

Select three sentences from a favorite book. Discuss punctuation, capitalization, and spelling of any unfamiliar words with your teacher. Identify nouns. Then copy the sentences on the lines below.

When you have finished, your teacher will dictate to you the same sentences for writing and grammar practice. [Please write dictated sentences on a separate sheet.] After your teacher has dictated these sentences to you, check your work by comparing it with the sentences in the book. Be sure to note capitalizations and punctuation. [If the teacher prefers, the student may read the sentences, slowly, into a digital recorder, then substitute the recording for teacher dictation.]

Be sure to turn to page 1 for more practice exercises.

My Journal Page

[Assign after page 80 has been completed.]

Write a sentence telling about a food you don't like. Include at least one contraction. Then write a few more sentences telling how you could make the food taste better. Circle the verbs in all the sentences.

Copywork and Dictation

[Assign after page 81 has been completed.]

Select three sentences from a favorite book. Discuss punctuation, capitalization, and spelling of any unfamiliar words with your teacher. Identify nouns. Then copy the sentences on the lines below.

When you have finished, your teacher will dictate to you the same sentences for writing and grammar practice. [Please write dictated sentences on a separate sheet.] After your teacher has dictated these sentences to you, check your work by comparing it with the sentences in the book. Be sure to note capitalizations and punctuation. [If the teacher prefers, the student may read the sentences, slowly, into a digital recorder, then substitute the recording for teacher dictation.]

Be sure to turn to page 1 for more practice exercises.

My Journal Page

[Assign after page 90 has been completed.]

Write a sentence telling what you had for breakfast. Include at least three nouns and three adjectives. Then write two sentences telling how the breakfast was prepared. When you are finished writing, underline the verbs, circle the nouns, and draw a box around the adjectives.

Copywork and Dictation

[Assign after page 91 has been completed.]

Select three sentences from a favorite book. Discuss punctuation, capitalization, and spelling of any unfamiliar words with your teacher. Identify nouns. Then copy the sentences on the lines below.

When you have finished, your teacher will dictate to you the same sentences for writing and grammar practice. [Please write dictated sentences on a separate sheet.] After your teacher has dictated these sentences to you, check your work by comparing it with the sentences in the book. Be sure to note capitalizations and punctuation. [If the teacher prefers, the student may read the sentences, slowly, into a digital recorder, then substitute the recording for teacher dictation.]

Be sure to turn to page 1 for more practice exercises.

My Journal Page

[Assign after page 100 has been completed.]

Write a few sentences telling about a priest in your parish. What does he look like? Is he tall or short? What does he do to show that he loves Jesus and His Church? When you are done writing, circle nouns, underline adjectives, and draw a box around pronouns.

Copywork and Dictation

[Assign after page 101 has been completed.]

Select three sentences from a favorite book. Discuss punctuation, capitalization, and spelling of any unfamiliar words with your teacher. Identify nouns. Then copy the sentences on the lines below.

When you have finished, your teacher will dictate to you the same sentences for writing and grammar practice. [Please write dictated sentences on a separate sheet.] After your teacher has dictated these sentences to you, check your work by comparing it with the sentences in the book. Be sure to note capitalizations and punctuation. [If the teacher prefers, the student may read the sentences, slowly, into a digital recorder, then substitute the recording for teacher dictation.]

Be sure to turn to page 1 for more practice exercises.

Answer Key

Language of GOD for Little Folks

Level B

Answer Key

p. 2
On Sunday we go to Holy Mass. We will meet Jesus there.

p. 3
All sentences end with periods.

p. 4
God made me to know Him, etc.
Chocolate ice cream tastes good.
Mittens make my hands feel toasty.
Last summer, my family camped in the mountains.

p. 5
A.
1. C
2. N
3. N
4. C
5. C
6. N
7. N
8. N
9. C
10. N
11. C

p. 6
A.
1. N
2. C
3. N
4. N
5. N
6. N
7. N
8. C
9. C
10. C
11. N

p. 7
A.
1. ...is made in the image...
2. ...think of others.
3. ...listened to God.
4. I can help to...
5. ...be ready for...

p. 8
All sentences should begin with a capital.

p. 9
Each sentence should begin with a circled word and end with a question mark.

p. 10
A.
1. ?
2. ?
3. ?
4. ?
5. .
6. .
7. ?
8. .
9. .
10. ?
11. .

p. 11
A.
1. .
2. .
3. .
4. ?
5. .
6. ?
7. ?
8. .
9. .
10. .
11. ?
Endings will vary.

p. 12
A.
1. T .
2. C .
3. Q ?
4. C .
5. C .
6. C .
7. Q ?

p. 13
A.
1. T .
2. C .
3. Q ?
4. C .
5. T .
6. T .
7. C .
8. C .
9. Q ?
10. C .
11. Q ?
12. C .
13. T .
14. T .

p. 14
A.
1. can
2. Can
3. may
4. may
5. may
6. May
7. can
8. may
9. can
10. May
11. may

p. 15
A.
1. C .
2. E !
3. E !
4. C .
5. C .
6. E !
7. E !
8. C .
9. C .
10. E !

p. 16
A.
1. C .
2. T .

3. T .
4. Q ?
5. E ! or T .
6. E ! or T .
7. E !
8. E !
9. C .
10. Q ?
11. C .
12. T .
13. T .
14. E !

p. 17
A.
School often starts...
Autumn leaves fall...
Honking geese begin...
Each season shows..
B.
1-5: All sentences should have the first letter circled and a capital letter printed above
1. ?
2. ?
3. .
4. .
5. .
6. Answers will vary.

p. 18
sniff
stroke
leap
hike
praise
believe
certain

p. 19
A.
1. silently
2. present
3. adore
4. shut
5. finished
B.
positive
raised
believe
loving

p. 20
A.
1. snoozing
2. infant
3. crib
B.
Answers will vary.

p. 21
dirty
take
sorrow
lose
early
awake
good
foolish

p. 22
A.
1. older
2. early
3. whispers
4. carefully
5. excited
B.
cooked—raw
false—true
slow—rapid
push—pull
strong—weak
mean—kind
follower—leader

p. 23
A.
1. Son
2. hear
3. be
4. dear
B.
brakes—used to stop a bike or car
breaks—damages or destroys
weak—not strong
week—a seven-day period
pear—a tasty fruit
pair—a group of two things
see—look
sea—ocean

p. 24
A.
flower
sock
girl
house
helmet
rollerblades
grandma
popsicle

p. 25
A. [Pronouns such as "he" and "Himself" do refer to persons, so give credit if your child circles them.]
1. child, priest
2. boy, confessional
3. kneeler, wood
4. chair, crucifix
5. boy, Jesus
6. God
7. man, house
B.
8. families, hillside, Jesus
9. Mothers, children, grass
10. stomachs, babies
11. people, lunch, food
12. boy, Jesus, basket, fish, rolls
13. Jesus, heaven, food
14. bread, hands
15. Jesus, men, women, children
16. Jesus, people, world, Bread

p. 26
~~boy~~, (Dan)
(Uncle Rick) ~~uncle~~, ~~hat~~
~~land~~, (Boston), ~~city~~
(Father Karl) ~~priest~~, ~~father~~
~~church~~, (Holy Name Church)
~~water~~, (Red River), ~~river~~

p. 27
A.
Answers will vary.
B. Proper nouns, in bold below, should be circled.
1. **Nathan, Marie**, parents, **Rome**
2. car, churches, **Tiber River**
[The pronoun "them" refers to people, so give credit if your child underlines it.]

3. city, statues, popes, saints
4. family **Pope Francis, Saint Peter's Church**

p. 28
A.
all capitals
B.
1. Jesus Christ, Lord, Savior, Redeemer
2. Holy Trinity, God, Father, God, Son, God, Holy Spirit
3. Son, Holy Spirit, God, Father

p. 29
A.
all capitals
B.
1. Mary, Mother, God, Son, Jesus, God, Son
2. Blessed Sacrament, Body, Christ

p. 30
A.
view
create
repair
B.
break
destroy
sunny
C.
sun
pear
D.
1. N
2. C
3. N
4. N
5. C

p. 31
A.
1. Q ?
2. C .
3. E !
4. Q ?
5. T .
B.
1. C
2. P
3. C

4. C
5. P
6. P
7. C
8. P
C.
1. I, Holy Trinity, Father, Son, Holy Spirit
2. Mary, Mother, God, Blessed Mother
3. Jesus, Lamb, God, Calvary

p. 32
A.
trees, keys, rocks, forks
B.
dresses, dishes, glasses, matches, foxes, branches

p. 33
1. trucks
2. beaches
3. classes
4. dishes
5. desks
6. carrots
7. dresses
8. shirts
9. chairs
10. foxes
11. papers
12. branches
13. patches
14. birds
15. cakes
16. letters
17. squashes

p. 34
A.
copies
cherries
skies
puppies
pennies
berries
B.
man—men
woman—women
goose—geese
foot—feet
sheep—sheep

tooth—teeth
deer—deer
child—children

p. 35
medals
fonts
bushes
churches
women
crutches
rosaries
watches
stamps
deer
geese
feet
puppies
brushes

p. 36
A. All should have 's.
B.
1. POS
2. PLU
3. POS
4. PLU
5. POS
6. PLU

p. 37
A.

King Darius had a wicked advisor who was jealous of Daniel. He was jealous of Daniel's wisdom. He and his nasty partners were also jealous of Daniel's friendship with the king.

This wicked advisor tricked the ruler into signing an order to trap Daniel. The king's order said that no one could pray to anyone but to him. Anyone who did not obey the king's decree would be thrown into a den of mean, hungry lions.

However, Daniel was God's servant. His prayers would be to God alone. One day, Daniel was faithfully praying inside his house. Daniel's window was wide open, so all who passed by could see Daniel praying.

Sadly, the (advisor's) plan worked. Daniel was caught, arrested, and cruelly tossed into the den of ~~lions~~. A huge stone was rolled in front of th(e den's o)pening, making escape impossible. As a roaring lion walked toward Daniel, Our Lord slammed th(e lion's m)outh shut. God was keeping Daniel safe even in the midst of wild b~~easts~~.

Meanwhile, King Darius, who was really (Daniel's) friend, also cried out to God to spare (Daniel's) life. Ho~~urs~~ later, when the king saw that Daniel was still alive, he ordered that Daniel be pulled out of the den.

King Darius saw that neither were (Daniel's) ~~bones~~ broken nor did he have any scr~~at~~ches on him, so he wrote a new order. The (ruler's) new decree was to all pe~~op~~les and na~~ti~~ons. It commanded worship of the true God, who has worked si~~gns~~ and wo~~nd~~ers in heaven and on earth, and who saved Daniel from the ja~~ws~~ of ~~lions~~.

p. 38
A.
1. trees
2. tree's
3. book's
4. books
5. Jesse's
6. skirts
7. skirt's
8. stones
9. St. Stephen's
B.
PLU
PLU
POS
POS
PLU

p. 39
A.
1. run
2. hop
3. jumping
4. sing
5. hit
6. pray
7. push
8. blowing

p. 40
A. ski, ride, hopping
B.
[Action words listed; all others should be crossed out.]
1. tiptoe
2. skip
3. splash
4. sleep
5. pray
6. pecking
7. sip
8. scrub

p. 41
A.
1. is
2. are
3. is
4. is
5. am
6. is
7. is
8. am
9. are

p. 42
A.
1. is
2. am
3. is
4. am
5. is
6. are
7. is
8. is
9. are
10. are
11. am

p. 43
A.
1. be
2. be
3. be
4. act
5. act
6. be
7. act
8. act
9. be
10. be
11. act
12. be
13. act
14. act

p. 44
A. **The words in bold below should be circled.**
1. be   **is**
2. be   **are**
3. act   **hunt**
4. be   **is**
5. be   **am**
6. act   **tiptoe**
7. act   **watch**
8. be   **are**
9. act   **flies**
10. be   **are**
11. be   **is**
12. be   **is**
13. be   **am**
14. act   **walk**

p. 45
A. **The words in bold below should be circled.**
1. now   **are**
2. now   **is**
3. now   **am**
B.
1. was
2. was
3. were
4. was
5. were

p. 46
A.
1. past   was
2. present   am
3. present   are
4. past   were
5. present   is
6. present   are
7. past   was
8. past   were
9. past   was
10. past   were
11. past   were
12. present   are
13. present   is

p. 47
Answers will vary.

p. 48
A.
[The words in bold below should be circled.]
1. **was** flying
2. **was** blowing
3. **were** racing
4. **is** cutting
5. **is** wiggling
6. **are** falling

B.
1. past   was talking
2. past   were cheering
3. present   is building
4. present   are studying
5. present   is forming
6. past   was taking
7. present   am sending

p. 49
A.
1. keys
2. beaches
3. cherries
4. branches
5. medals
6. kitties
7. rocks
8. guesses
9. foxes
10. feet
11. geese
12. berries

B.
Rose's
Noah's
boy's

p. 50
A.
sailing
swim
fishing
cook
eating
pour

B.
1. was sailing
2. were wrecking
3. swam
4. was built
5. threw
6. was bitten
7. shook
8. was protecting

p. 51
A.
1. fill
2. fills
3. carries
4. carry
5. roll
6. rolls
7. jumps
8. cuts
9. feed
10. feeds
11. commands
12. gives

p. 52
A.
1. yes
2. no
3. yes
4. yes
5. yes
6. no
7. yes
8. no
9. no
10. yes

p. 53
A.
1. have
2. has
3. have
4. have
5. have
6. has
7. have

p. 54
A.
1. have
2. have
3. has
4. has
5. have
6. have
7. has
8. has
9. has
10. has
11. has
12. has
13. has
14. have
15. have

p. 55
Add -ed to all.

p. 56
A.
sing—sang
eat—ate
sit—sat
write—wrote
sleep—slept
drink—drank
see—saw
run—ran

p. 57
A.
[Words in bold below should be circled.]
1. **has** prayed
2. **have** slept
3. **has** given
4. **has** hurt
5. **have** arrested

6. **have** taken
7. **has** washed
8. **has** lifted
9. **has** fallen
10. **has** cared
11. **has** helped
12. **has** wiped
13. **has** blessed

p. 58
A.
[Words in bold below should be circled.]
1. was
2. **had** come
3. **had** hoped
4. **had** waited
5. **have** travelled
6. opened
7. **had** handed
8. **was** praising
9. **had** found
10. **have** found

p. 59
A.
1. went
2. gone
3. done
4. go
5. did
6. done
7. do

p. 60
A. [Words in bold below should be circled.]
1. present **is** making
2. present cuts
3. present **are** sorted
4. past **has** mailed
5. past made
6. past **have** finished
7. past **were** praying
8. past went
9. past **have** done
10. present **am** starting

p. 61
A.
1. An angel
2. The children
3. The angel
4. The angel
5. The little shepherds
6. Her heart
7. A pearl rosary
8. The Lady
9. God

p. 62
A.
1. The Hebrews
2. Cruel Pharaoh
3. The Hebrew slaves
4. Tall pyramids
5. The hot sun
6. Desert winds
7. The people
8. Moses
9. The rivers
10. Bugs
11. Frogs
12. Pharaoh
13. The Angel of Death
14. God's children
15. God

p. 63
A.
1. burned in the desert.
2. spoke from the bush.
3. had suffered.
4. was stubborn.
5. chased the Hebrews.
6. opened up.
7. walked safely to the other side.
8. took God's people to the Promised Land.

p. 64
Sentences may be in any order.
The sleepy cat yawned and stretched.
My new bike was speeding down the hill.
Jesse's warm hat was pulled over my ears.
Lucy's doll is in the dollhouse.
That peanut butter sandwich filled my stomach.

p. 65
A.
1. grew up in Albania.
2. loved Our Lord very much.
3. had died.
4. opened a store.
5. sold cloth in the store.
6. worked hard.
7. helped teach little students.
8. invited her to visit.
9. wanted to serve God as a nun.
10. travelled to India.
11. wanted to serve the poor.
12. gave his blessing.
[St. Teresa of Calcutta]

p. 66
A.
[More than one answer possible for all; answers may vary.]
1. Agnes and her brother Lazar went on a picnic.
2. Lazar ran down the hill and rolled in the grass.
3. Agnes picked wildflowers and gave them to her mother.

p. 67
[More than one answer possible for all; answers may vary.]
1. St. Paul and Silas were in jail.
2. St. Paul was praying and singing joyfully.
3. The jailer and his family asked to be baptized.

p. 68
Stories will vary.

p. 69
Stories will vary.

p. 70
A.
1. cry, eat
2. make, sit, kick
3. break, leap
B.
1. are
2. am
3. is

C.
1. dog's collar
2. cats have fur
3. pair of glasses
4. two dogs
5. horse's mane
6. Dad's glasses
7. Father's house
8. frogs in the pond
9. cat's fur

D.
1. C
2. C
3. P
4. P
5. P
6. C

p. 71
A.
1. S
2. S
3. A
4. S
5. A

B.
[Words in bold below should be circled.]
1. present — **are** starting
2. past — **has** mixed
3. past — finished
4. present — **is** taking

C.
1. Beth, Carmen, Bramble Road
2. I, First Holy Communion, Holy Name Church
3. My, Uncle Jack, Lincoln, Nebraska.

p. 72
1. jumping
2. praying
3. pushed
4. bumped

B.
passing, passed
blessing, blessed
reaching, reached
smelling, smelled
greeting, greeted
talking, talked
walking, walked

p. 73
A.
1. popping
2. skipped
3. stopped
4. dripping

B.
tapping, tapped
stepping, stepped
pinning, pinned
slipping, slipped
snapping, snapped
begging, begged
batting, batted

p. 74
A.
1. farming
2. wished
3. milked
4. matching
5. dressing
6. dragged
7. sledding
8. bragged

B.
trapping, trapped
leaping, leaped
licking, licked
slipping, slipped
clapping, clapped
bagging, bagged
starting, started

p. 75
A.
1. live
2. hope
3. adore
4. praise

B.
loving, loved
baking, baked
promising, promised
caring, cared
gluing, glued
taping, taped
racing, raced

p. 76
A.
1. pasted
2. biking
3. wrapping
4. fasted
5. wiping
6. whipped
7. living
8. fasting
9. pasting
10. praised
11. setting
12. sledded

B.
slide—root that ends with signal -e...
hop—short vowel/single consonant end...
start—root that doesn't change...

p. 77
A.
1. untrue
2. reopen
3. untold
4. undo
5. distrust
3. retold

B.
reclose
disobey
remake
unopened
unheard

p. 78
A.
1. unseen
2. unable
3. dislike
4. redo
5. dishonest
6. repay

B.
refold
unhappy
retry
unkind
unseen

p. 79
A.
would not
did not
is not
let us
was not

p. 80
A.
1. didn't
2. hasn't
3. Let's
4. shouldn't
5. isn't
6. wasn't
7. aren't

p. 81
A.
2—driving
1—eat
2—napkin
1—sing
2—later
1—sheep
2—Maker
2—holy
1—saint
B.
r<u>ea</u>d
g<u>ar</u>den
st<u>u</u>dent
p<u>o</u>p
h<u>i</u>s
sp<u>ee</u>d

p. 82
A.
1. trust
2. west
3. fast
4. dry
5. fight
6. free
7. pin
8. blood
9. still
10. bail
11. letter
12. praise

p. 83
A.
play—1
day—1
between—2
unseen—2
B.
side—guide
star—far
child—mild
bed—head
praise—raise
be—me
C.
guide
me

p. 85
A.
1—bread
1—bake
2—baker
1—pan
2—cupcake
1—ram
1—lost
2—shepherd
1—find
2—comfort
1—net
1—boat
2—fishing
2—river
1—hook
B.
b<u>ab</u>y
sl<u>e</u>epy
<u>a</u>ngel
w<u>a</u>tch
beds<u>i</u>de
<u>g</u>uard
La<u>d</u>y
f<u>ai</u>th
Vir<u>g</u>in
p<u>u</u>re
M<u>o</u>ther
h<u>o</u>ly
p<u>o</u>pe
l<u>ea</u>der
ch<u>u</u>rch
spe<u>a</u>k
l<u>i</u>sten
<u>o</u>b<u>e</u>y

p. 86
A.
[Words in bold below should be circled.]
1. **tiny** <u>baby</u>, **lacy** <u>bonnet</u>
2. <u>baby</u>, **white** <u>dress</u>, <u>baptism</u>
[Baptism is a noun, but may be difficult for student to recognize as a person, place or thing. Explain that student can check its 'noun-ness' by demonstrating that adjective modifiers can be attached to the word. For example, *happy* baptism, *holy* baptism, *short* baptism, *quiet* baptism.]
3. **Cool** <u>water</u>, **little** <u>forehead</u>
4. **soft** <u>skin</u>, **quiet** <u>infant</u>
5. <u>Mary Katherine</u>, **sweet** <u>baby</u>, **beautiful** <u>soul</u>
B.
[Only adjectives are listed; other words should be crossed out.]
hot
tasty, sticky
scratchy, blue
holy
funny
squeaky

p. 87
[Words in bold below should be circled.
Pronouns such as "she," "he," and "we" do refer to persons, so give credit if your child underlines them.]
1. <u>Nick</u>, **busy**, <u>family</u>
2. **happy** <u>family</u>, **huge** <u>farm</u>
3. **little** <u>brother</u>, **plump** <u>pigs</u>
4. <u>Nick</u> **heavy** <u>buckets</u>, **cracked** <u>corn</u>, <u>pen</u>
5. **older** <u>sister</u>, **red** <u>hens</u>
6. **fresh** <u>eggs</u>, **old, tin** <u>pan</u>
7. <u>Mother</u>, **brown** <u>eggs</u>, **shiny** <u>skillet</u>
8. <u>family</u>, **hot** <u>breakfast</u>
9. <u>Nick</u> **young** <u>calves</u>
10. **warm** <u>milk</u>, **metal** <u>pail</u>
11. <u>Nick</u> **hard** <u>floor</u>, **old** <u>barn</u>
12. **greedy** <u>calves</u>
13. **Sticky** <u>milk</u>, **blue** <u>jeans</u>
14. **Clean, dry** <u>hay</u>, **wooden** <u>manger</u>
15. **tasty** <u>meal</u>, **good** <u>God</u>
16. <u>God</u>, **strong** <u>families</u>, <u>farm</u>

145

p. 88
Stories will vary.

p. 89
A.
1. faster
2. fastest
3. brighter
4. tallest
5. kindest

p. 90
A.
1. shorter
2. shortest
3. louder
4. closest
5. smallest
6. highest
7. longer
8. safest
9. closer
10. finer

p. 91
A.
1. past
2. past
3. present
4. past
5. present
B.
1. Our Lord
2. tells his sins to the priest.
3. has made a good confession.
C.
[Words in bold below should be circled.]
1. **had** asked
2. **has** said
3. went

p. 92
A.
1. (burn)ing
2. (pump)ed
3. (climb)ing
4. (call)ed

B.
5. spraying
6. dragging
7. dripping
8. slipping
C.
replay
reprint
remake
reopen
D.
unlike or dislike
undo
E.
1. 1
2. 1
3. 2
4. 2
5. 1
6. 2

p. 93
A.
1. He
2. Him
3. his
4. It
5. them
6. He
7. their
8. they, him

p. 94
A.
1. yes, He
2. no
3. yes, His
4. yes, Him
5. no
6. yes, Thee, Thy
7. yes, Thy, Thy

p. 95
A.
1. I
2. me
3. I
4. me
5. me
6. I
7. I

p. 96
A.
1. We
2. us
3. them
4. They
5. They
6. them
7. us
8. we

p. 97
A.
1. more   You
2. one   You
3. one   You
B.
1. She
2. He, her, His
3. they
4. Him
5. us
6. We
7. They [or We]
8. them [or us]

p. 98
A.
1. We
2. us
3. They
B.
1. It
2. us
3. They
4. his, her
5. She, him
6. They
7. them, Him

p. 99
January—Jan.
February—Feb.
March—Mar.
April—Apr.
May—May
June—June
July—July
August—Aug.
September—Sept.
October—Oct.
November—Nov.
December—Dec.

Sunday—Sun.
Monday—Mon.
Tuesday—Tues.
Wednesday—Wed.
Thursday—Thurs.
Friday—Fri.
Saturday—Sat.

p. 100
1. Jan.
2. May
3. Sun.
4. Wed.
5. June
6. Mar.
7. Mon.
8. Oct.
9. Nov.
10. Tues.
11. Dec.
12. Aug.
13. Feb.
14. Apr.

p. 101
A.
1. St.
2. St., St.
3. St.
4. Rd.
5. N., St.
6. E. St.
7. Bl.

p. 102
A.
Sister—Sr.
Father—Fr.
Doctor—Dr.
Missus—Mrs.
Miss—Miss
Mister—Mr.
B.
1. Mrs.
2. Sr.
3. Dr.
4. Mr.
5. Fr.

p. 103
A. Answers will vary.
B.
Jesus, Mary, Joseph—J.M.J.
Ad Majorem Dei Gloriam—
   A.M.D.G.
My God, I Love Thee—
   M.G.I.L.T.
All for Thee, Dear Jesus—
   A.F.T.D.J.

p. 104
Mr. Daniel Aranda
1302 Mountain St.
Lebanon, OR 55379

p. 105
A.
The student's address should be written in the upper left corner. The envelope should be addressed to:
Mrs. Mary Tillotson
2320 Brownbush Rd.
Skey, MO 07794

B.
The student's address should be written in the upper left corner. The envelope should be addressed to the student's grandparents.

p. 106
Letters will vary.

p. 107
A.
<u>Saints of Ireland</u>
Fr. Patrick Kiernan
B. Titles and authors of favorite books will vary.

p. 108
A.
1. 2
2. 17
3. 12
4. 22
5. 15

p. 109
baptized
convert
Ireland
miracles
Patrick
shamrock
Trinity

p. 110
A.
lady
least
life
Lourdes
B.
Fatima
field
flames
friends
C.
after
angel
ask

p. 111
A.
damp
dog
drink
B.
wagon
wet
wipe
wrist
C.
baby
birth
bless
born
D.
Mary
medal
miracle
Mother
E.
candy
cookies
cracker
cupcake

147

p. 112
1. mouth
2. sit
3. smile
4. meal
5. tent
6. trip

p. 113
page #1
1. scrape
2. seed
3. ship
4. skate
page #2
1. soap
2. spark
3. squash
4. stop

p. 114
1. His
2. us
3. We
4. us
5. They
6. them
B
1. I
2. me
3. She
4. I
C.
1. [none]
2. His
3. Thy

p. 115
1. Aug.
2. Fr., MI
3. Mr.
4. St.
5. St.
6. Rd, N. E.
B.
The Children of Fatima
The King of the Golden City
Little House on the Prairie
The Little Princess